IRIS MURDOCH, MURIEL SPARK, AND JOHN FOWLES

IRIS MURDOCH, MURIEL SPARK, AND JOHN FOWLES

DIDACTIC DEMONS
IN
MODERN FICTION

Richard C. Kane

Rutherford ● Madison ● Teaneck
Fairleigh Dickinson University Press
London and Toronto: Associated University Presses

© 1988 by Associated University Presses

Associated University Presses
440 Forsgate Drive
Cranbury, NJ 08512

Associated University Presses
25 Sicilian Avenue
London WC1A 2QH, England

Associated University Presses
P.O. Box 488, Port Credit
Mississauga, Ontario
Canada L5G 4M2

The paper used in this publication meets the requirements
of the American National Standard for Permanence of Paper
for Printed Library Materials Z39.48-1984.

Library of Congress Cataloging-in-Publication Data

Kane, Richard C. (Richard Charles)
    Iris Murdoch, Muriel Spark, and John Fowles.

    Bibliography: p.
    Includes index.
    1. English fiction—20th century—History and
criticism.   2. Didactic fiction, English—History and
criticism.   3. Demonology in literature.   4. Murdoch,
Iris—Criticism and interpretation.   5. Spark, Muriel—
Criticism and interpretation.   6. Fowles, John,
1926–   —Criticism and interpretation.   7. Good and
evil in literature.   8. Fantastic, The (Aesthetics),
in literature.   I. Title.
PR888.D53K36   1988   823'.914'09353   87-45754
ISBN 0–8386–3324–2 (alk. paper)

PRINTED IN THE UNITED STATES OF AMERICA

To my parents,
Edward and Loretta Kane

CONTENTS

ACKNOWLEDGMENTS

I wish to thank Richard Kennedy from Temple University for reading chapters of the book and making helpful comments at various stages of its composition. I am also indebted to friends and colleagues at the Mont Alto Campus of Penn State University: the cooperative librarians; my conscientious typist, Vicki Sprenkle; George Payette and several interested faculty members, but especially Martha A. Fisher of the English department, who gave the enthusiastic advice that could come only from another fan of Murdoch and Fowles. My greatest personal debt is to Lee Feltwell whose love and intelligence helped me wrestle with more than one demon that has sprung up beside the twisting route to a final manuscript.

Lastly I would like to thank Iris Murdoch, Muriel Spark, John Fowles and the following publishers for allowing me to use copyright material:

Viking Penguin Inc. and Chatto and Windus Ltd. for permission to quote from Iris Murdoch's *The Flight from the Enchanter, A Severed Head,* and *The Unicorn;* Harold Ober Associates Limited for permission to quote from Muriel Spark's *The Ballad of Peckham Rye* (Copyright © 1960, 1988 by Copyright Administration Limited), *The Public Image* (Copyright © 1968 by Copyright Administration Limited), *Not to Disturb* (Copyright © 1971 by Copyright Administration Limited); and finally, Little, Brown and Company and Anthony Sheil Associates Ltd. for permission to quote from *The Collector* by John Fowles (Copyright © 1963 by John Fowles, Ltd.) and *The Magus: A Revised Version* by John Fowles (Copyright © 1977 by John Fowles Ltd.).

OVERVIEW

What do you expect of a spiritualist? His mind's attuned to
the ghouls of the air all day long. How can he be expected to
consider the moral obligations of the flesh?
—Muriel Spark, *The Bachelors*

An intriguing phenomenon to emerge in several postwar British authors
is the odd combination of the moral and the macabre. Demonic personalities dominate a fiction charged with strong didactic currents. Searching for the good within the realms of the grotesque, Iris Murdoch,
Muriel Spark, and John Fowles make significant moral statements by
using a variety of demonic elements.

Iris Murdoch's shadowy world, for instance, includes the following
characters: an exotic European with one blue eye and one brown eye
who demonstrates a special talent for mesmerizing his "creatures" into
subservience; an anthropologist who swings a Samurai sword and transforms a polite historian into a kicking madman; and a retired playwright
so entranced with his fantasy about the lost love of his youth that he
kidnaps her when he finds her at the seashore forty years later, even
though in addition to seashells she has accumulated wrinkles, a mus-
tache, and a violent husband (*The Flight from the Enchanter*, *A Severed
Head*, and *The Sea, The Sea*). Murdoch's obsessed characters often circu-
late within eerie settings such as Gothic mansions, underground tunnels,
labyrinthian cellars, and desolate seascapes. Some of the most uncanny
events, however, take place in public libraries, hospital wards, or on city
fire escapes as Murdoch reveals her keen sense of the unexpected in the
midst of the commonplace. Sensational events laced with lurid trappings
can also color her work: Black Masses, dead pigeons, whips, chains,
suicide, murder, and mutilation are all to be found in a novel called *The
Nice and the Good*.

Strange events and characters are similarly woven into the fine fiction
of Muriel Spark, who has been described as an author with one foot off
the ground.[1] "It is all demonology," says one of her characters.[2] Indeed,
unusual personalities do flit about like wraiths—especially through the
narrow halls of Spark's more recent fiction. *The Hothouse by the East River*
is inhabited by a neurotic whose shadow falls in the wrong direction and

who sits by the window hour after hour "seeing things." In *The Driver's Seat* a woman screams in disapproval when she learns that the gaudy dress she is about to buy will not show the blood stains she plans to produce during an appointment with her murderer. And in *Not to Disturb* a group of ghoulish servants make elaborate plans with the media to sell the sensational "inside" story of their masters' imminent murder-suicide, which they have also helped arrange; meanwhile, thunder rolls, lightning cracks, and "him in the attic" lurches about in lusty madness.

Besides Murdoch and Spark, John Fowles has on occasion marched in this Halloween parade. Just as kidnapping becomes the central event in several of Murdoch's works, Fowles's first novel describes a slightly deviant young man who progresses from collecting butterflies to bottling up beautiful young women. In one of the selections from *The Ebony Tower* an elderly scholar receives a nocturnal visit from an unusual burglar whom the scholar soon refers to as "my young demon." And in *The Magus* a remote Greek island forms the backdrop for sorcery, sadism, and a pageant of grotesques in an eerie mingling of fact and fantasy.

Along with their interest in the demonic, however, Murdoch, Spark, and Fowles also seem firmly committed to exploring their characters' ethical dimensions. In a number of her philosophical essays, Iris Murdoch explains that moral activity depends upon constant attention to the otherness of people who are not ourselves. The problem results when we impose fantastic forms or concepts upon contingent reality, including other real people. Just as dominant types will mold more formless beings into servile dependency, so too will those in need of a controlling power often enslave themselves to an enchanter figure. We thus frequently create our own demons. Murdoch recognizes that art itself can become a type of enchantment, "a temptation to impose form where perhaps it isn't always appropriate."[3] Thus the creation of art becomes a type of moral activity, as the novelist must constantly try to recognize contingency and construct a "house fit for free characters."[4] Murdoch acknowledges that as an artist she has sometimes been unable to resist the temptations of form.

Muriel Spark also has expressed an interest in moral philosophy. In an essay on her religious beliefs, Spark states that her career as a novelist began only after her conversion to Roman Catholicism. Although she does not want to belabor this sequence, she admits that her religion has provided her with a type of ground work from which to write. But as Karl Malkoff has said about Spark's fiction, "God is seen through a glass darkly, if . . . at all."[5] Muriel Spark has explained that fiction to her is "a kind of parable."[6] Although in *The Public Image* she explores a Murdochian situation where the myth of a celebrity becomes more vital than the actual woman, frequently Spark uses different moral strategies. Not unlike some of T. S. Eliot's poetic maneuvers, one of Spark's novelistic techniques is to create clear, sharp images of a moral wasteland, where the ethical statement is expressed more by what is missing than by what is present. Death-in-life situations, and characters who are often more spectral than human, underline the qualities of compassion and integrity by their conspicuous absence.

In *The Aristos*, John Fowles elucidates certain ethical ideas that inform his fictional world. Like Spark, he calls one of his novels a "parable," and like Murdoch, he sees the danger in imposing a rigid form on shapeless reality. He too recognizes the dangers of labeling and categorizing when "everything is unique in its own existing."[7] In *The Collector* Frederick Clegg fails to perceive this uniqueness when he mumbles that the best photographs of the naked Miranda were those in which the camera cut off her head. Instead of an individual being, Miranda has become a replaceable object, whose form happens to be Clegg's obsession. Miranda too, for all her pseudo-liberal jargon, really fails (in the Murdochian terminology) to "attend to" Clegg as a unique individual who exists separately from her conception of him as a bourgeois bumpkin. When he tells her his name is Ferdinand, she immediately substitutes the label "Caliban" and continues to think of him as such for the rest of the novel. Lastly, in *The Magus* Fowles's cryptic old teacher, like Murdoch's anthropologist, employs magical techniques ultimately to disintoxicate the young protagonist from the illusions he himself has created to avoid a direct confrontation with earthy reality.

For Fowles too, aesthetic concerns become ethical concerns. Like Murdoch, he has seen the dangers of form. In *The Aristos*, he writes, "Form is a death sentence, matter is eternal life."[8] Perhaps even more than Murdoch, Fowles tries to free his characters from older aesthetic conceptions.

To clarify the use of the demonic by these didactic writers, one might briefly look at an earlier author who has been considered both preacher and devil. In her book *Pan the Goat-god: His Myth in Modern Times*, Patricia Merivale sees the culmination of the Pan myth in the first half of the twentieth century in the fiction of D. H. Lawrence. Indeed, Lawrence's dark heroes and violent horses do resemble sinister Pan-figures as they crash through the artificial barriers civilized society has built to restrain the vital rhythms passing through the cosmos. However, with Lawrence the crashing activity becomes positive destruction: in order for the new to live, the old must be torn away. Lawrence urged modern men and women to smash the rotting framework of civilization in order to discover tenderness in the human heart. Thus in Lawrence, demonic associations are almost always positive. Primitive destructive forces are needed to free mankind from the shackles of civilization.

Although certain creations of the three contemporary authors are shaded with this more positive demonic element, much more frequently the demonic takes on decidedly negative connotations. In works such as *The Flight From the Enchanter, The Unicorn, A Fairly Honourable Defeat, The Sea, The Sea, The Public Image, The Hot House by the East River, The Collector,* and *The Magus,* true evil results when individuals are locked inside rigid concepts that become fantastic in their incongruity with the relatively formless beings inside struggling to be free. One might think, for example, of the desperation of Hannah Crean-Smith in Iris Murdoch's *The Unicorn* as the layers of the terrible myth surrounding Gaze Castle envelop her more and more firmly. In this work the real demons are artificial concepts imposed upon other individuals. Humans must be disintoxicated from these demonic distortions in order to be truly moral and alive.

In one sense, then, Pan has been tamed. One might hesitate to use such sweeping terms as "the new morality" or perhaps "a rediscovered morality" to describe the didactic impulses of a number of postwar writers. Yet, unlike the preoccupations of formalism, there does seem to be an increasingly orthodox concern for one's fellow man that also differs from the fiery religion of sex that Lawrence was preaching. The didactic intent of these more recent writers is to rout the demons—even though they use methods that themselves often seem diabolic. As one of Muriel Spark's odd characters announces: "I have the powers of exorcism . . . the ability to drive devils out of people." Reflecting upon this young man's frequent reports that the bumps on his head were caused by the surgical removal of horns, his friend states, "I thought you were a devil yourself." The young man—both demonic and didactic—replies, "The two states are not incompatible."9

In exploring the fiction of Iris Murdoch, Muriel Spark, and John Fowles, I will therefore examine the connections between the fantastic fringes and moral centers of their novels. Although many of their works combine the demonic and the didactic, I have focused on particular novels in which this strange combination can be most clearly observed.

IRIS MURDOCH,
MURIEL SPARK,
AND JOHN FOWLES

PART I

Iris Murdoch

SPELLBOUND
The Flight from the Enchanter

Although many critics praise the realistic London scenes and whimsical charm of *Under the Net,* readers do not reach the mysterious heart of Murdochland until they explore the author's second novel. In *The Flight from the Enchanter* the writer blends magic and morality to prepare her special brew.

Essentially a didactic work, the novel examines the evil that can develop when fantasy is imposed upon human relationships. The rigid distortions that result often evolve into a type of demonic power. Since the sources of these powerful distortions are often complex, Murdoch creates an intentional ambiguity that confused some of the novel's earlier readers such as Olga Meidner[1] and William Van O'Connor, who found the "book's diverse meanings hard to perceive."[2]

One clue to this work ignored by almost all the critics lies in its dedication to the Nobel-prize novelist and sociologist, Elias Canetti, who serves as a prototype for several philosophical figures in Murdoch's fiction, especially Willy Kost in *The Nice and the Good.* Although Murdoch did not review *Crowds and Power* until the English translation appeared in 1962, Canetti started writing his masterpiece in 1948, and as one of his few close friends, Murdoch was undoubtedly familiar with his thought. One scholar's description of *Crowds and Power* as "an account of the psychology and structure of authority"[3] could also be applied to *The Flight from the Enchanter,* which analyzes the strange influence a powerful figure named Mischa Fox exerts over a variety of people. In the second part of *Crowds and Power,* which studies the psychology of the despot, Canetti writes that "Secrecy lies at the very core of power."[4] Looking at Murdoch's fictitious despot, we learn that aside from his reputation as a wealthy international press lord whose influence seeps over continents, Mischa Fox is shrouded in secrecy. The civil servant Rainborough muses:

No one knows Mischa's age. One can hardly make a guess. It's uncanny. He could be thirty, he could be fifty-five. . . . No one knows where he came from either. Where was he born? What blood is in his veins? No one knows. And if you try to imagine you are paralyzed. It's like that thing with his eyes. You can't look into his eyes. You have to look at his eyes. Heaven knows what you'd see if you looked in.[5]

So too Canetti writes: "Power is impenetrable. One man who has it sees through other men but does not allow them to see through him" (*CP*, 292). To make her secret potentate even more exotic, Murdoch paints one of Mischa's eyes brown and the other blue, suggesting that her enchanter can wear different faces for different occasions with no one view of him being correct. The novel's shifting point of view offers a variety of interpretations of this complex figure, but the one unexplored mind is Mischa's. This conspicuous omission, of course, cultivates the aura of secrecy surrounding the title character. The reader learns of rumors and fables that have sprung up around his name, and the man himself finally appears in the seventh chapter, but never do we enter Mischa's own mind.

Canetti has also described the paranoia of the autocrat, who closets himself behind walls of protection: "No one may come near him; a messenger, or any one who has to approach him, is searched for weapons" (*CP*, 232). One of the characters in Murdoch's novel contemplates a similar difficulty involved in approaching the cryptic press lord:

> Ringing up Mischa was always a discouraging experience. Half a dozen different voices might be heard at the other end of the line. . . . They were anonymous voices by whom the caller was interrogated, stripped and often finally rejected. (*FE*, 292–93)

Besides secrecy and remoteness, a third quality of both Canetti's and Murdoch's despots is the ability to wait. Canetti sees the tyrant as a predator whose authority depends upon power over life and death. Frequently the tyrant imitates the watching beast who secretly lies in wait for his prey: "And in order to achieve success in the end the watcher must be capable of endless patience" (*CP*, 290). Canetti's words sound strikingly like those of the Murdochian character who explains: "There's only one thing that's exceptional about Mischa, apart from his eyes, and that's his patience. He always has a hundred schemes on hand, and he's the only man I know who will wait literally for years for even a trivial plan to mature" (*FE*, 134).

Canetti writes that when the despot lies in wait, "he knows what he is watching for and knows, too, which of his creatures he can use to help him" (*CP*, 292). Murdoch also employs the term "creatures" to describe those individuals whose obedience to Mischa seems absolute, such as Nina the dressmaker and Mischa's henchman, Calvin Blick (*FE*, 154). Blick's pornographic photographs and insidious blackmailing techniques echo Canetti's description of the "filing system of secrets" used by the tyrant and his aides as an instrument of control (*CP,* 292). More parallels could be drawn. Written only a few years after Hitler's rise to power, Canetti's book assumes enormous political significance. As he himself says, "It is only a step from the primitive medicine-man to the paranoiac and from both of them to the despot of history" (*CP,* 292). Reflecting the author's experiences with the war refugees she encountered in her job at the United Nations Relief and Rehabiliation Administration (UNRRA) from 1942 to 1946, *The Flight from the Enchanter* represents one of Murdoch's most political novels.

Besides Canetti and her own wartime experiences, another important influence on the book was the French mystical philosopher Simone Weil, who starved herself to death during World War II because she refused to eat any more food than what she thought available to those in occupied France. As Edmund Campion has written, "This immolation was the climax to a lifetime's desire to share the harshness and brutalities of the lives of the poor."[6] Interestingly, Susan Sontag sees a strong correspondence between Weil, "another expert on power," and Canetti, in "the force of his testimony to the ethical necessity of siding with the humiliated and the powerless."[7]

Weil emphasizes the inherently evil nature of power itself. In "Analysis of Oppression" she writes, "There is, in the very essence of power, a fundamental contradiction that prevents it from ever existing in the true sense of the word; those who are called masters, ceaselessly compelled to reinforce their power for fear of seeing it snatched away from them, are forever seeking a dominion essentially impossible to attain."[8] In Murdoch's novel, Mischa and his men unravel elaborate schemes to gain control of the *Artemis,* the relatively powerless feminist magazine that has long since lost the force and scope intended by its founders.

Weil also applies her theories on power to the personal realm, "where love . . . destroys all balance in the soul as soon as it seeks to dominate or to be dominated by its object."[9] Her term "attention" means the constant awareness we must have of the otherness of people who are not ourselves. Having acknowledged Weil's influence in her article, "Against Dryness,"[10] Murdoch also uses "attend" and "see" to describe patient, careful observation of other people's reality. Her term "enchantment" characterizes the process whereby attention gives way to fantasy and preconceived forms are imposed upon contingent human beings. Fantasy becomes demonic when both people in a relationship give in to imaginary distortions. Servile creatures bow to their demonic masters, who reinforce the fantasies of their slaves. Murdoch often assumes the didactic task of demonstrating the illusory nature of this demonic power.

Discussion of Canetti, Weil, refugees, slaves, and demons might suggest that Murdoch has written a very grim book populated by a fiery

tyrant equipped with boots and chains and followed by a band of soldiers, rigid with slavish obedience. But this image would not be accurate.
Mischa himself, for instance, often seems to embody childlike innocence
and charm; sometimes he even sits on the floor with his legs curled up
under him. Much of the fascination of Murdoch's work lies in its delicate
exploration of the shadowy border between domination and submission.
The book considers the degree of choice involved in servitude: to what
extent does the slave fly from the demonic master and to what extent
does he embrace him?

Murdoch's name for her central character incorporates this ambivalence. Although a fox is a predatory animal, it is also preyed upon by
man. Indeed, many of the novel's characters seem to spend a good deal
of time tracking down, chasing, or "hunting" Mr. Fox. The more one
reads the more one wonders, for instance, if the frail managing editor,
curiously called Hunter Keepe, really wants to rescue the *Artemis* from
the clutches of Mr. Fox.

Like the wild animals depicted on the draperies in Mischa's mansion,
all three names—Fox, Hunter, and Artemis—suggest the motif of flight
and pursuit that involves so many of the characters in the book's pan-
oramic view of society and serves as a metaphor for demonic obsession.

One of the most persistent pursuers is Annette Cockayne, a nineteen-
year-old whose jet-set parents have stashed her away in a girls' finishing
school in London. In the light comic strokes of Chapter One, Murdoch
foreshadows the whole theme of enchantment while sketching Annette
as she drops out of school.

Annette's inclination to use fantasy as a means of escape from unpleasant situations is shown when she ignores classroom lectures by either
daydreaming or slipping into a "self-induced coma of stupidity" (*FE,* 9).
During one of her reveries, Annette decides that she will educate herself
in the "School of Life" rather than the finishing school of Miss Walpole.
As she makes her grand exit, Annette resembles a dreamlike figure.
Stealing a souvenir from the school library, she moves silently under a
"delicious spell" (*FE,* 10). Like another famous dreamer, "It was as if she
had walked through the looking glass. She realized that she was free"
(*FE,* 9). As she defiantly swings from the chandelier in the school dining
hall, she falls "into a sort of trance" (*FE,* 11). The fluffy vision of
Annette's wonderland momentarily dissolves, however, when she slips
from the chandelier and crashes to the floor at Miss Walpole's feet, thus
giving her ritual of "dropping out" a delightfully literal significance.

Annette's fantasies become more dangerous when she focuses them
upon a man, but through a series of flashbacks Murdoch first shows why
Annette will be especially vulnerable to Mischa's power. The child of a
diplomat, Annette was raised in a hectic world full of fast trains and

"badinage in four languages" (*FE*, 61). Shuttled through a childhood whose boundaries were constantly shifting, this emotional refugee has become a flightly, impetuous girl whose divergent energies nevertheless seem to cry out for some implacable form. Demonstrating this need, she habitually "places" people in relation to herself, a process dependent on her knowledge of the other person's "exact age" (*FE*, 82). She then often casts the person in her own private drama, turning her dressmaker Nina, for example, into a "superior sort of lady's maid" (*FE*, 81).

It is during a fitting in Nina's dressmaking shop that Annette finally encounters the individual who will act as a catalyst to her volatile personality. The scene ripples with imagery reflecting the book's major themes:

> Nina stood back for a moment, the pins still in her mouth, to survey her work in the glass. It was then that Annette realized that someone had entered the room. A man had come in and was standing by the door at the far end of the lane of clothes. Annette could see him in the mirror. She could see their three heads, her own bright and close, Nina's below her, a little in shadow, and the man's head, far back over her shoulder, and quite darkened. Yet she knew that he was looking into her eyes. (*FE*, 85)

The dominant symbol of the looking glass reinforces the Alice-in-Wonderland motif. The fact that Annette sees Mischa for the first time in a mirror suggests that he too will become a reflection of her private fantasies. On the other hand, Fox does seem ominous as he steps back "into the shadow of the hanging clothes and stands there like a man on the edge of a forest" (*FE*, 86).

Although Annette tries to be informal with Mischa, she is soon disturbed by his own casual attitude: "He was clearly not exerting himself. He was simply watching her, as one might watch a bird" (*FE*, 87). Her physical situation of being a model for an unfinished dress predicts the way she will allow herself to become a pawn in an imaginary drama: "Suddenly now Annette felt helpless. Nina was moving her arms and her head about as if she were made of wood. She felt like a puppet" (*FE*, 86). When she finally is dressed in her own clothes again, Annette searches frantically in her handbag partly to keep busy and partly to find "some charm against the incomprehensible pain of the present moment." Is Mischa enchanting Annette, or is she allowing herself to be mesmerized by her own fantasies of this mysterious man, whose "face was in shadow again" (*FE*, 86)? The subtle imagery of mirrors, shadows, and forests suggests that both processes are at work.

This strange interplay continues: in a later scene Mischa gains seductive power as for the second time he appears while Annette is partially undressed. This time her blouse has been ripped off by Rainborough,

Mischa's acquaintance whom Annette has visited in order to find out more about Mischa. Attracted to Annette, Rainborough is tussling with her on the floor when Mischa suddenly enters his hallway. Afraid of scandal, Rainborough has just enough time to stuff both Annette and her blouse into the china cupboard. During the following scene Mischa resembles an amused god playing with mortals as he toys with Annette's scarf and stares directly at the china cupboard while casually sitting in conversation with Rainborough, who wriggles in discomfort. Annette's stifling physical incarceration replicates the emotional confinement she will suffer through her obsession with Mischa, who relishes the power he gains over the two embarrassed victims by his unexpected visit. The cupboard scene recalls Murdoch's frequent use of tight, enclosed areas as symbols of neurotic, self-absorbing fantasies, such as the hall closet with a peep hole in *The Time of the Angels* and the subterranean cell in *Henry and Cato*.

Annette's attraction to Mischa grows so intense that one night after a wild party, she stalks him in the streets, following after him, "softly, resolutely, tenderly, like a hunter" (*FE*, 214). But as she approaches him, it is with a "mixture of terror and triumph" (*FE*, 214).

Her debilitating obsession with Mischa at one point leads to a suicide attempt. Instead of sleeping pills, however, she mistakenly swallows dozens of milk of magnesia tablets with a lot of gin. Although the results prove comic, her self-destructive tendencies are nonetheless real. But Murdoch gives Annette a youthful resiliency that unfortunately a number of the other characters do not share.

One such character is Nina, the dressmaker. When Annette first sees Mischa in the mirror, the pins Nina uses to hold together the unfinished dress nicely suggest the influence Mischa will exert on each of the women: a few pins only "prick" Annette's flesh, but when Nina rubs her hand across her mouth that holds several more pins, she draws blood. If Annette is a bird that momentarily diverts Mischa's attention, Nina is one that he has actually encaged. A real rather than spiritual refugee, Nina has "no official existence" since her passport was issued by a Foreign Office that "had disappeared from the face of the earth" (*FE*, 289). Even more than Annette's, Nina's life lacks definition and form, a fact that Murdoch emphasizes by not assigning her a surname but by frequently referring to her as Nina, the dressmaker, as if she must earn her identity by her occupation. As a result of her formless existence, Nina becomes more vulnerable to the enchanter's power than Annette:

When Mischa had appeared in [Nina's] life she could, from the first moment, have refused him nothing. He bore with him the signs of a great authority and carried in his indefinable foreignness a kind of oriental magic. She was ready from the first to be his slave. . . . (*FE*, 151)

Mischa installs Nina in a shop in Chelsea and sends her enough customers so that she enjoys a modest reputation. But when she wants to expand her business by hiring helpers, Mischa disapproves. Her mysterious role requires that she live alone: at a moment's notice, for instance, she must provide overnight accommodations to anonymous guests bearing notes from Mischa.

As the secretive nature of the relationship intensifies, what Nina thought was love for Mischa is gradually transformed into "a strange emotion which had in it more of terror and fascination than of tenderness" (*FE*, 154).

The "iron discretion" that Mischa imposes upon Nina's life makes isolation the key condition of her existence. Alone, she becomes more susceptible to the fears that initially drew her to Mischa. When she learns she is regarded as only one of dozens of "creatures" that Mischa has enslaved, she secretly plans to flee to Australia. Afraid of officialdom, she tries to enlist the services of Rosa Keepe, one of her few friends who also has known Mischa. But the three times that she approaches Rosa, her friend is so absorbed in her own problems that she scarcely notices the distressed seamstress. When fears of being arrested because of illegal residency couple with her complex feelings about Mischa, Nina decides that she can escape only through the "frontier where no papers are asked for" (*FE*, 290), and while Annette failed in crossing this mysterious border, Nina sadly succeeds.

It is somewhat ironic that Rosa never helps Nina because Rosa herself has also been enthralled by the inscrutable Mischa Fox—and in more complicated ways than were either of the other two women. Ten years earlier Rosa ostensibly terminated an intense relationship with Mischa, yet she remains acutely aware of his strange influence and feels uneasy whenever Mischa returns to London. At one point Rosa thinks about Mischa: "It made no difference. Whether she ran towards him or away it was all the same" (*FE*, 282).

The daughter of a zealous feminist who helped found the *Artemis*, Rosa herself has never passionately struggled for any particular cause. She allows her brother to manage the feminist magazine that she has inherited, illustrating her indifference to her mother's strong principles. Rosa's upper-class education allows her to dabble at journalism and to teach at a girls' school for a while, but she finally gets a job in a factory in a mood of self-conscious asceticism, wanting work that is unpretentious and dull. The passages that describe Rosa's succumbing to the hypnotic sound of the machines "whose rhythm . . . filled her body" show that she as well as Annette occasionally induces a numbing mindlessness.

Her tendency to slip into states of extreme passivity gets her into trouble with the Lusiewicz brothers, two Polish immigrants at the factory where she works. It is the dilemma created by her relationship with the two handsome young foreigners that ultimately leads her back to Mischa. She doesn't know that Mischa's henchman, Calvin Blick, learns of the relationship and even photographs her with the brothers before she herself decides to turn to Mischa for help, a knowledge that adds to Mischa's omniscience since Rosa had gone to great lengths to keep the affair secret.

Rosa's entanglement with the Lusiewicz brothers is tinged with that bizarre coloration that has become Murdoch's special hue. When the brothers first arrive at the factory, they remind Rosa of two "half-starved, half-drowned animals." She secretly adopts them, tutors them, and nourishes their almost magical transformation into attractive young workers, popular with the ladies because of their virile good looks and with the men because of their mechanical skill and willingness to learn. At first all the power belongs to Rosa, for Jan and Stefan Lusiewicz:

> made no choice without her opinion, they were her slaves. Rosa feared this power, but she enjoyed it too. There were days when, contemplating the grace and vitality of her protégés, she felt as if she had received a pair of young leopards as a present. It was impossible not to adore them, it was impossible not to be pleased to own them. . . . (FE, 49)

For a time Rosa keeps her fantasy neatly contained within definite parameters, symbolized by the "enchanted circle" where the trio sit for English lessons in the middle of an empty bed frame in the brothers' cheap room in Pimlico.

Adding to the bizarre atmosphere, the boys' toothless mother sits eternally silent amidst a bundle of rags in the far corner of the L-shaped room. Although the situation is strange, as long as Rosa can stay in control and maintain the secrecy of the relationship by never allowing the brothers to visit her home, she continues to enjoy her authority over these two primitives who occasionally dance wildly about the room for her.

But the power shifts when one evening while escorting Rosa, Stefan begins to moan passionately. Aware of his intense physical desire, Rosa slips into "a coma of misery" because she does not want to turn brother against brother. She soon finds herself "secretly hoping that in some way the brothers would take over the situation and make all the necessary decisions for her" (FE, 58). This is exactly what happens as Jan and Stefan initiate the ritual of "taking turns." After the English lessons are over, on alternate evenings each brother makes savage love to Rosa on the floor in the middle of the empty bed frame as the old mother quietly looks on.

The English lessons continue although they are now surrounded by an even more fabulous aura, with strange looks and double meanings interjected between the rules of grammar. One evening as the brothers quietly approach Rosa, "their smiles hovered over her like two angels" while Rosa looks up "allowing herself to be spellbound" (*FE*, 70). As the mastery passes to the Lusiewicz brothers, Rosa grows more and more uneasy, and "as the days passed she began to fear them" (*FE*, 60). One evening the brothers tell her a primitive tale from their native East European village about their own transformation from the obedient students of a pretty young school teacher to her phantom lovers who ultimately destroy her, a tale that nearly charts the course the brothers will travel with Rosa herself. In one scene, while Jan lies with his head in Rosa's lap, he "looked up at her, and his eyes upside down were the eyes of a demon" (*FE*, 79).

The influence of the brothers spreads like a shadow over Rosa's life: "The darkness in which those two held her was profound beyond the reach of names. She could not of her own will break the spell" (*FE*, 110). Soon these shadowy aliens fly out of the "enchanted circle" at Pimlico and begin to haunt Rosa's house at Campden Hill Square. Gradually, Stefan announces that he is moving in. After a diabolic scene, where this demonic twin terrifies Rosa's sensitive young brother by setting his hair on fire, Rosa decides to approach Mischa Fox—feeling that only "darkness could cast out darkness" (*FE*, 256).

Like a moth darting about a flame, Rosa makes her decisions with great trepidation. She decides, for instance, to tell Mischa only about the problem of Stefan and keep the intimate details of her relationship with the two brothers an absolute secret, for such knowledge would put Mischa "in possession of a weapon against Rosa of such power that she grew pale at the thought of any person ever possessing it, let alone using it" (*FE*, 110). But in spite of one moment's great reluctance, at another moment Rosa seems absolutely compelled: "She knew that even if Mischa were oblivious of her existence, yet he was drawing her all the same. She was reminded of stories of love philtres which will draw the loved one over mountains and across the seas" (*FE*, 257). In her decision to see Mischa, Rosa realizes she obeys the "demon of unreason" and acts as if "under a spell" (*FE*, 257).

Recalling the looking glass imagery in Annette's initial encounter with Mischa and reinforcing the solipsistic theme, Rosa's first reunion with Mischa in his London mansion "was like looking into a mirror. It was as if her own spirit had imprinted itself upon him as they embraced and now looked back at her wide-eyed" (FE, 262). Although the couple laugh and kiss, and finally Mischa promises to help with the problem of her uninvited guest Stefan Lusiewicz, at the end of the interview Rosa notices a subtle shift of atmosphere:

> There was a demon in Mischa which she had never been able to know and which had never allowed them to be at peace. Always at the last moment and without apparent reason, there would come the twist, the assertion of power, the hint of a complexity that was beyond her, the sense of being, after all that had passed between them, a pawn in Mischa's game. . . . (FE, 263)

Yet Mischa's demon is not the only one to which Rosa must attend. Although she feels that she is selling herself into captivity, Rosa thinks "to be at [Mischa's] mercy was at that time her most profound desire. If there had been a fire between them she would have leapt into it" (FE, 263).

Through friends in Parliament, Mischa sees to it that the problem of illegal aliens gets considerable notoriety and almost immediately Stefan Lusiewicz vanishes. But one problem in Rosa's life has dissolved only to be replaced by another: "Reflection and counter-reflection about Mischa Fox had brought her to a point of disequilibrium where rest was no longer possible" (FE, 292). Although Rosa tries to resume normal activities in a life without Mischa, who has retreated to Italy, she cannot function very effectively. Murdoch uses expressionistic landscape to capture Rosa's obsession: as she is walking one night, "Rosa had never in her life noticed so many telephone boxes. They stretched before her like monoliths that mark the way to a temple; in each one of them a picture of Mischa Fox was hanging up" (FE, 292). Although she cannot get Mischa on the phone, she finally decides to storm the temple itself and make the long journey to Mischa's Italian villa, since "it now seemed to her that she had always known that it was a place to which she would go" (FE, 294).

The chapter describing the final encounter between Rosa and Mischa shimmers like a mirage in its surrealistic imagery, paralleling the illusory nature of their relationship. Rosa's blurred vision caused first by the dazzling sunlight outside and then by the dark, shuttered rooms within corresponds to her inability to see Mischa clearly. Her feeling of insecurity is heightened by the shifting perspectives of the chapter, such as her sudden awareness that the patio floor beneath her is alive with struggling insects or the shocking realization that Mischa, far below her on the beach, has uncannily spotted her looking at him through a pair of binoculars. The strangeness is compounded by grotesque images, such as a lizard whose tail comes off in Rosa's hand.

Just as Rosa is about to join Mischa on the beach, Calvin Blick intervenes, first telling Rosa of Nina's suicide and then showing her his sensational photograph of her in the arms of the Lusiewicz brothers. Calvin succeeds in making Rosa feel guilty about not helping Nina, who would only have had to fill out a few more forms to avoid being arrested. He also frightens Rosa with the thought of the absolute power over her the photograph would give Mischa. He never reveals, however, whether he acted on his own or under Mischa's orders in taking the photograph. Adding to the unreal aura, Calvin then tells Rosa: "You will never know the truth, and you will read the signs in accordance with your deepest wishes. That is what we humans always have to do. Reality is a cipher with many solutions, all of them right ones" (*FE,* 304–5). Her sense of reality shaken to the core, Rosa once again flees from the enchanter.

Although Annette, Nina, and Rosa are in varying degrees enslaved by Mischa Fox, the enchanter's influence is by no means limited to women. Mysteriously attracted to Mischa, Rosa's sensitive younger brother felt more frustrated than anyone when years earlier Rosa rejected Mischa, suggesting that Hunter had intended to use his sister to explore vicariously his own feelings for the powerful press lord. Yet Hunter wants to protect Rosa from any form of evil—even if it comes from Mischa. To suggest the ambivalence of Hunter's attitude toward the enchanter, Murdoch employs patterns of imagery similar to those used for a number of the other characters. In one scene, for instance, mirror imagery suggests the solipsistic theme when Hunter combs his hair in a shop's glass door, only to perceive that he is suddenly transformed into Mischa's henchman, Calvin Blick, who it turns out is actually standing on the other side of the door. The paradoxical flight-pursuit motif is reinforced when later in the same scene, Hunter accuses Mischa's agent of following him when in fact he is out of breath from chasing Calvin (*FE,* 169). Teasingly Murdoch allows both interpretations as she explains that Hunter, who loves detective films, often fancies he's being followed and then writes the scene as if Calvin is indeed pursuing Hunter to attract his attention so that he can ultimately lure him down into Mischa's dark basement.

Calvin Blick himself provides an example of a soul totally dominated by the will of the enchanter. Disgusted with Calvin's treacherous methods of blackmail, Rosa cooly says to him, "I cannot think why Mischa has not killed you years ago." Showing the absolute state of his subjection, Calvin softly replies, "Mischa did kill me years ago" (*FE,* 306). As Calvin leads Hunter into the labyrinthian cellar of Mischa's urban mansion, he resembles the Minotaur, a horrible monster created by Mischa to do his dirty work. With its tubs of bubbling solutions the damp cellar serves both as Calvin's photographic studio and as the Gothic setting for the diabolic drama that follows. Sadistically Calvin tricks Hunter into helping him develop a particular photograph. Equipped with tongs, Hunter holds the unrevealed photo in a bubbling solution, but as a picture of his sister writhing in the arms of the Lusiewicz brothers gradually whirls into existence, Hunter suddenly drops the tongs and screams at Calvin, "You devil!" (*FE,* 174).

Just like the expensive instruments he uses, Calvin too serves as Mischa's machine. As Calvin holds up the "large crystalline object," he says, "This is my eye. . . . This is the truthful eye that sees and remembers. The lens of my camera. You couldn't buy an eye like this for five hundred pounds" (*FE,* 172). Calvin's photographs parallel the crystalline aesthetic object Murdoch has written about in that they both attempt to impose rigid forms upon contingent reality. In its static display a photograph catches a segment of life but freezes it and thus reduces it, just as Calvin tried to reduce the complex personality of Rosa into an unchangeable sexual object in a dirty picture. As the photographer attempts to encase life in a type of permanent form, so does the demonic mind try to confine reality in a permanent form; the docile slave seeks out the static situation of obedience to a fixed will while the demonic master sees a changeable human being only as a steady tool. Demonic enchantment excludes the contingent aspect of personality just as a photograph excludes fluid reality. When Calvin says the camera is his eye, he reveals his own limited vision. Enslaved to Mischa, he is no longer a changeable human being, but a fixed agent, like a machine or a camera. Calvin's predetermined role is suggested by his very name.

The novel's more diabolic scenes, such as this subterranean encounter between Hunter and Calvin, are tempered by some of the more comic episodes involving figures such as Rainborough and his aggressive secretary Agnes Casement, whose capers provide, as Frank Baldanza has noted, a "realistic mooring" for some of the more fantastic adventures in the rest of the book.[11] And although many of the novel's characters seem to be molded by the will of others, a few prickly individuals emerge. The only real opposition to Mischa Fox's attempt to take over the *Artemis* comes in the form of a group of aging but wealthy suffragettes led by the cantankerous Camilla Wingfield, an old eccentric whose last name suggests freedom and whose first name suggests the violence needed to attain that freedom in that it recalls the ax-wielding huntress who was a favorite of the legendary Artemis.[12] Thus the opponent of evil is herself no sunny personality. The rich old lady laughs "fiendishly" (*FE,* 121), abuses her servant-companion, becomes obnoxious with any visitors, and boasts of "doing-in" her husband with a flat-iron. In her indifference about her appearance, her defiance of convention, and her candid speech, Camilla Wingfield anticipates the equally strange Honor Klein, another Nietzschean scourge, in Murdoch's fifth novel.[13] Camilla

Wingfield represents the vital force needed to destroy the illusory worlds formed by so many of the other characters in the novel. The raucous scene where Camilla and her gang of harpies swoop down upon the board meeting of the *Artemis* just in time to rescue the magazine from the crafty Fox provides one of the novel's few signs of hope and suggests that the demonic process of enchantment can be resisted with a realistic appraisal of the situation. At one point in the meeting the effete Hunter Keepe starts mumbling, for instance:

> "It's a matter of financial necessity. . . . Perhaps I can explain."
> "They need cash!" shouted Mrs. Wingfield. (*FE*, 186)

Although the feminist theme looms large in this chapter, Murdoch prevents the whole episode from becoming tendentious by her skillful use of humor. When one old lady finally realizes that Mischa Fox wants to seize control of the journal, she asks:

> . . . "do I understand you to say that it is proposed to sell the *Artemis* to—a man?"
> Hunter gestured hopelessly. "I've been running this thing for two years now . . . and after all I'm a man!" A stiff silence followed this shameless declaration. (*FE*, 186)

Even though Camilla Wingfield does serve as an astringent needed to treat the ailments caused by fantasy and illusion, her power is severely qualified by her age and by the fact that she dies before the novel ends.

Another potential source of light in the fog of illusion that envelops so many of the other characters is the scholar Peter Saward, who has gained a special insight into life perhaps because he has come so close to death. Since he has lived with advanced but quiescent tuberculosis, Saward has become "in some profound way looser, less rigid" (*FE*, 30–31). Although his body degenerates, his spirit soars as he grows strangely cheerful. Part of his strength comes from an objective mind that remains open to others. Rainborough muses about Saward, for example, "Here was a personality without frontiers. Saward did not defend himself by placing others" (*FE*, 34). Since Saward thinks that even the odious Calvin Blick has a "pleasant smile" (*FE*, 37), Rosa tells Peter that sometimes his good nature "approaches imbecility" (*FE*, 37).

Peter Saward turns out to be one of the few characters who can begin to unveil the layers of mystery surrounding Mischa Fox, who visits the scholarly recluse regularly. During one visit Mischa tells of a childhood fair where all the children in the town were given little one-day old chickens that everyone knew would shortly die. Since Mischa felt great sadness for all helpless animals, he would sometimes take it upon himself to kill these creatures before they could be destroyed by some other means. He tells Peter how he once even killed a little kitten he had received as a gift. As Mischa talks to Peter, the scholar reflects "how strangely close to each other in this man lay the springs of cruelty and of pity" (*FE*, 225). Peter Saward, who reminds one of Elias Canetti, studies Mischa just as he studies an ancient code he tries to decipher throughout the novel:

> He looked at Mischa, feeling again the puzzlement and tenderness with which these curious encounters always filled him. Mischa was a problem which, he felt he would never solve—and this although he had got perhaps more data for its solution than any other living being. Yet it seemed that the more Mischa indulged his impulse to reveal himself in these unexpected ways to Peter, the more puzzling he seemed to become. . . . (*FE*, 223–24)

Although he is a serious scholar, Saward's power as a seer is undermined in several ways, such as the satiric description of his cluttered room that "must have contained some 3000 volumes of which at least a hundred were open, some lying horizontal, some at an angle of forty-five degrees, and others vertical, opened at a favorite illustration and perched on top of bookshelves or supported ingeniously by pieces of string" (*FE*, 23). Saward becomes "fanatically systematic" in his monumental effort to decipher the ancient code, at one point even devising an ambitious method where he could utilize all twenty-four hours of the day by taking notes in the dark on any thoughts that might come to him during his sleep. During one of his daytime study sessions, Saward "had laid his pen aside and was looking gloomily at the sheets of hieroglyphics. They were as impenetrable as ever. At last he stacked them into a neat pile" (*FE*, 222). The neat pile suggests the form that man tries to impose upon what is essentially unknowable and formless. By the end of the novel a bilingual text is discovered near Tarsus that proves that all of Saward's scholarly clues were wrong and that all of his years of research were wasted.

Although Saward's experience with the ancient code seems to symbolize futility, it can paradoxically be read in a more positive way if the ancient code is seen as a symbol of the complex, impenetrable nature of the human personality. The mysterious code becomes especially positive if contrasted to Calvin Blick's photography that attempts to contract the human personality into a knowable fixed object.

Just as Peter cannot decipher the code, so too he cannot "decipher" Mischa. But unlike what he tries to do with the code and unlike what so many of the characters try to do with Mischa, Saward does not as a result of this mystery try to impose a "private reading" upon his friend; he does not assign Mischa a role in an imaginary drama. His restraint leads to a saner relationship. After a wild party where Annette attacks Rosa in a fit of jealousy over Mischa, Mischa says to Peter, "Everybody has been going mad. . . ."

Peter replies, "You make them mad."
Mischa counters, "I don't make you mad." (*FE, 222*)

The demonic distortions do, however, seem, to cast shadows over most of the characters. After Rosa flees from Mischa's Italian villa, for instance, her first stop in London is Peter Saward's room. Although Mischa has consulted Saward several times, Saward has remained relatively immune from Mischa's power because of his objective mind and his absorption in academic interests. But in an attempt to distract the agitated Rosa, Saward happens to pick up an album of photographs of the childhood village of none other than the ubiquitous Mischa Fox, whose influence once again looms like a gray cloud over Rosa's life as well as the novel's final scene.

The last chapter seems even more unsettling in light of an earlier episode in which Rosa had mulled over Mischa's knowledge of her relationship with Peter. Wondering what new scheme Mischa had in mind, Rosa felt "as if Mischa were pressing the suit of Peter Saward, although nothing had been said which could unambiguously be read in this way. What does he want? . . . Does he want to keep Peter and me together in a cage" (*FE, 282*)? Rosa also entertains the thought that Mischa's nudging her toward Peter might merely be an attempt to make Rosa disgusted with the preoccupied scholar and therefore ultimately draw her to Mischa himself. Another enigma arises when it occurs to Rosa that "she was . . . singularly without information about the relations of Mischa and Peter" (*FE, 282*).

The final scene leaves the reader with a sense of irresolution. Instead of experiencing a satisfying denouement or unraveling, one feels only further ensnared by the labyrinthian network of relationships. In her didactic task of demonstrating how easily one can slip into a chrysalis of demonic illusion, Murdoch herself becomes the ultimate enchanter.

2

PHANTOM PROFESSOR
A Severed Head

While *The Flight from the Enchanter* surveyed a wide spectrum of society, Murdoch's next novel to search for the moral in decidedly macabre realms focuses on a much smaller cast of characters, all of whom belong to the somewhat intellectual upper middle class. Another striking difference is that the multiple point of view of the earlier novel is replaced by a curious first-person narrator. But in no other work by Iris Murdoch does the demonic seem more didactic than in *A Severed Head*. Her fifth novel, in fact, traces the education of a protagonist by a forceful teacher whose eerie influence upon her student disturbs him profoundly. Before the terrible lessons begin, however, the author makes clear the necessity of instruction.

Murdoch's decision to allow Martin Lynch-Gibbon to tell his own story seems especially appropriate for a novel that criticizes self-absorption and the consequent failure to "see" the uniqueness of other individuals. On one level the novel delineates Martin's attempt to break out of his own solipsistic point of view. In the opening scene with his mistress Georgie, for instance, Martin admits to himself that he more or less phases her out of existence when he is not with her.[1] When later interests develop, he says, "I could not *see* Georgie anymore" (*SH,* 189).

Linda Kuehl has argued that Murdoch's division of characters into the enchanters and the enchanted "make(s) up a scheme symptomatic of the author's failure to break away from the tyranny of form."[2] In her discussion of *A Severed Head* the critic sees Martin as one of the enchanted victims; however, she never mentions Georgie Hands in the entire article. Kuehl has failed to recognize Murdoch's complexity of characterization. Although Martin seems more like a victim in various other relationships in the book, with Georgie he rules like a tyrant. In the opening scene she actually prostrates herself before him, laying her head upon his feet. Martin especially likes the "dry way in which [Georgie] accepted our relationship" (*SH,* 3). Martin has virtually turned his liaison with Georgie into the type of crystalline aesthetic object that Murdoch attacks in her essay, "Against Dryness." Georgie submits to the rigid form of the relationship carefully prescribed by Martin. Georgie has become Martin's pretty bauble, the secret plaything for whom he likes to buy barbarous necklaces, purple underwear, and black openwork tights. The clandestine nature of the relationship must be preserved; Georgie predicts that "if it were exposed to daylight, it would crumble to pieces" (*SH*, 13). People as well as novels then can suffer from a sense of formal closure. Having locked up Georgie in an airtight concept, Martin blinks in contentment over his impression that her apartment with its "warming murmuring fire" seems like "a subterranean place, remote, enclosed, hidden" (*SH*, 12).

Since Georgie serves as Martin's toy, the novel perhaps appropriately begins during the Christmas season, but this celebration of a famous birth assumes grimly ironic overtones when we learn that Georgie has had an abortion. Although responsible for the pregnancy, Martin has been let off easily by his secret mistress, who throughout the ordeal remained "calm, laconic, matter-of-fact" (*SH*, 13). We are told that it "had all been quite uncannily painless"—for Martin, that is. The messy contingency of an unwanted child is dealt with as Georgie remains true to the crystalline form of the relationship.

Georgie's toughness and dryness are complemented by the "dewy radiance" of Martin's wife Antonia. While he loves Georgie with a certain "cheerful brutality," he has established a "more decorous . . . essentially sweeter relationship with Antonia" (*SH*, 21). If Georgie is slightly messy, Antonia is meticulously concerned about appearances; while Georgie wears her hair in a "chaotic bun" (*SH*, 79), Antonia's hair is fashioned in a "neat golden ball" (*SH*, 56). Georgie's scraggly pieces of holly similarly contrast with Antonia's "dark evergreens tied with various clever sprays . . . of red and silver ribbon" (*SH*, 23). If Georgie is laconic, Antonia is loquacious. Having roots in Bloomsbury, garrulous Antonia believes all people should aspire to something called "a perfect communion of souls." Her particular creed is described as "a metaphysic of the drawing room" (*SH*, 18). If Georgie, a twenty-five-year-old graduate student, seems like a daughter to the forty-one-year-old Martin, Antonia, five years older than Martin, has "more than once" been mistaken for his mother (*SH*, 16). Martin has achieved a formal stasis in his two relationships: "I needed both of them, and having both I possessed the world" (*SH*, 21). With sloppy Georgie and fastidious Antonia, Martin Lynch-Gibbon, wine merchant and amateur historian, has seemingly reconciled his Dionysian and Apollonian impulses.

Both relationships prove false, however, because Martin has failed to attend to the real otherness of each woman. He has imposed his own fantastic shapes upon them and has turned them into so many ornaments on a Christmas tree. If Georgie suggests some cheap and curious trinket, Antonia, frequently associated with gold, seems like a "rich gilded object" (*SH*, 17).

Martin's delicately balanced holiday arrangement is upset when over cocktails one evening Antonia announces that for once she has been doing more than talking to her psychiatrist, Palmer Anderson. They have become lovers and Antonia wants a divorce.

Now roles are reversed and this time Martin becomes somewhat enchanted with both Antonia and Palmer, who as an old friend of the family possesses a certain attractiveness for the protagonist. The book begins to take on a surrealistic glow as Martin indicates: "the evening of Antonia's revelation . . . seemed in retrospect a lurid dream, full of ghoulish configurations and yet somehow mysteriously painless" (*SH*, 37). If ghostly figures begin to populate the novel, they are at least friendly ghosts. In fact, Palmer and Antonia desperately want everyone to remain very friendly: they wish to take Martin in, adopt him as it were, into their new family. "My child, my dear child," coos Antonia. Martin's new "parents" create a pleasant appearance: the aging yet still golden Antonia blends nicely with fifty-year-old, "beautifully cultivated" Palmer Anderson, whose "round head," "soft . . . silver-grey hair," and "smooth," young-looking face (*SH*, 19) all suggest a lifetime of calming people down. Faced with this smiling twosome, Martin cooperates. He is mesmerized by his wife and her analyst, a "modern magician" (*SH*, 20), into his "role of taking it well" (*SH*, 34). He conveniently agrees to move out of the family home and into an apartment, although he will always be a welcome guest at Palmer and Antonia's cheerful residence. He even realizes that the pleasant type of nightmare he is living can be thought of as being rather ordinary: he is simply being "coaxed along to accept an unpleasant truth in a civilized and rational way" (*SH*, 31). But although "good manners . . . assumed the air of a major virtue" (*SH*, 20), Martin learns that gentility does not equal goodness. And this hard lesson is taught to him by a ghostly personality who seems anything but friendly.

Since Antonia doesn't want Palmer to go out into the bad weather with a cold, Martin kindly agrees to drive to the train station to meet Palmer's half sister Honor Klein. Shrouded in fog and smelling of sulphur and brimstone, Liverpool Street Station reminds Martin of an "image of hell" (*SH*, 62). In the midst of this smoky inferno, the sinister figure of Honor Klein slowly appears.

In contrast to the soft smooth surfaces of Antonia and Palmer, Honor Klein is described in images of hardness and sharpness. Her "curving lips [are] combined with a formidable straightness and narrowness of the eyes and mouth." She flashes Martin a "keen look" when he first speaks to this "haggard" woman (*SH*, 64). Later she actually slashes about with a "hideously sharp" Samurai sword (*SH*, 118). Unlike the golden aura surrounding Antonia and Palmer, darkness frequently looms about Honor: she has "short black hair" and "narrow dark eyes" (*SH*, 64). At one point her features remind Martin of a face in a "Spanish religious painting, something looking out of darkness, barbarous yet highly conscious" (*SH*, 134). In still another scene Martin suffers from the "illusion that [Honor's] entire face . . . had become black" (*SH*, 134). Finally Palmer and Antonia's smiles have been replaced by Honor's "hint of insolence" (*SH*, 63), "surly" looks (*SH*, 134), and "something animal-like and repellent in that glistening stare" (*SH*, 64).

At the hellish station the didactic demon swiftly sets to work by remarking, "This is an unexpected courtesy, Mr. Lynch-Gibbon" (*SH*, 64). Only gradually does Martin realize the scorn behind her remark: it indeed seems odd for a man to be running errands for his wife's lover.

As Honor catapults herself into the cozy world of Antonia and Palmer, "the golden pair by the fire," Martin momentarily sees Honor as "some insolent and powerful captain . . . booted and spurred" (*SH*, 67–68). An earlier reference was made to this formidable don of anthropology who carries "many guns" (*SH*, 6). Ultimately Honor teaches Martin to become a fighter as well, since no good can come from "letting people off" (*SH*, 77). As the novel progresses, Honor's assault becomes more direct. In Laurentian tones she tells Martin that he is a violent man who can no longer "cheat the dark gods" (*SH*, 76). By gentleness he only prolongs this "enchantment of untruth" that Palmer and Antonia have woven around him. She insists that eventually he will "have to become a centaur and kick [his] way out" (*SH*, 76).

The strange professor must turn Martin himself into a demon in order to draw him out of Antonia and Palmer's "region of fantasy" and return him to the "real world" (*SH*, 70). Martin's education then resembles the underworld journey required of the mythic hero before he could reach his true destination: man must descend into the nightmarish hell of his subconscious mind before he can discover true reality.

Honor serves as Martin's hellish guide. Through her devilish intervention, for instance, Palmer and Antonia find out about the relationship between Martin and Georgie. Although temporarily upset, Antonia and Palmer soon bestow blessings and soon want to adopt both Martin and Georgie into their loving circle. Martin becomes increasingly frustrated as now both he and Georgie are "stroked and cosseted" in Palmer and Antonia's "benevolent imagination" (*SH*, 98).

Although she weeps and wails during her first encounter with Georgie, Antonia shows her true feelings—or lack of them—when after dinner that evening she and Palmer run off to the opera. While A. S. Byatt feels that the sword scene that follows seems too richly a setpiece, the somewhat encapsulated force of the episode is needed to pierce the cocoon of happy hypocrisy that Antonia and Palmer have been merrily spinning about all of the central characters. Faintly resembling the lacerating "Rabbit" chapter of Lawrence's *Women in Love,* the episode plunges into the subconscious world. And as Alan Friedman argues about Lawrence,[4] the slightly inflated imagery here could be defended as an objective correlative for the unconscious states of mind being explored. The scene forcefully depicts the transfer of demonic energy.

On New Year's Eve Martin calls at Palmer's residence, where a "yellow sulphurous haze" encases the street lamps (*SH,* 110). He finds the happy couple out, but comes across Honor Klein in the dining room which seems so "abnormally dark" that Martin wonders if some of the fog has not drifted in. He soon realizes that Honor has lapsed into an extreme state, although he does not know the cause of her agitation. Certainly looking like a fiendish instructor, Honor sits at the head of the table with a sharp Samurai sword that she has removed from the dining room wall. An expert with the weapon, she tells Martin that sword play in Japan is considered a spiritual exercise expressing control and power. Although the title of the book reverberates in various ways throughout the entire novel, one particular meaning is reinforced in this scene as Honor stands up and tosses first Antonia's and then Palmer's soiled dinner napkins into the air. Swiftly wielding the mighty weapon, Honor "decapitates" each napkin and then looks down at the "severed" remains (*SH,* 117). The dirty napkins represent Antonia's and Palmer's crumpled gentility. As the demonic Honor Klein slashes the symbol of their civilized mentality, she creates for Martin a terrifying demonstration of naked power. Soon the novice "experiences an intense desire to take the sword from her," as church bells signal the approach of the New Year.

Martin, however, does not immediately act upon the dark knowledge gained during this strange lesson. In fact, several evenings later while slightly drunk, he even seems to fall back into his submissive role as he serves wine to Antonia and Palmer in bed together in Palmer's exotic chambers. The "ecclesiastical candlesticks," the "gilded roses," the "rosy Persian rugs upon the white Indian-carpet," and Palmer's "cream-colored embroidered robe of Chinese silk" (*SH,* 128), all spin together into a sweet world of fantasy from which Martin must be disenchanted. Showing that Honor's violent lesson has had some impact, Martin at least spills the wine, making a "big red stain [that] spreads on the white absorbent carpet" (*SH,* 130) and that represents his suppressed violence.

The entire house, in fact, becomes symbolic. The psychiatrist's rosy, exotic bedroom suggests what Lawrence called "sex-in-the-head"—erotic activity that is self-conscious, detached, and ultimately trivial. Similarly, Martin's journey into the cellar with a heavy wine crate reminds one of a descent into the subconscious mind, the dark basement where primitive and demonic forces are unleashed. As Martin swears and stumbles about, he is suddenly interrupted by Honor Klein, "looking down at [him] broodingly." The didactic taunting continues as she labels him "the knight of infinite humiliation" (*SH*, 133). This time, however, the lesson hits home. The polite historian suddenly acts as if he is indeed possessed by a demon. He knocks Honor onto the cellar floor, jumps on her, and belts her across the face three times. Although she struggles "like a maniac" (*SH*, 135), her fiendish pupil cannot be overcome. But when Martin's temporary madness ends, Honor Klein quietly glides out into the fog once again.

The scene is quintessential Murdoch—apparently inexplicable, irrational, violent, demonic, and subliminally sexual. But one senses that somehow all the hard violence in the dark cellar is more sane and healthy than the sentimental slush drifting about in the posh bedroom upstairs.

Before too long Martin realizes he desperately loves Honor Klein, whose image becomes "vast across [his] way as the horizon itself or the spread wings of Satan" (*SH*, 150). His nightmarish compulsion for her makes his two previous relationships resemble pleasant daydreams: "how flimsy these other attachments seemed by comparison. The power that held me now was like nothing I had ever known" (*SH*, 152). He is truly possessed. Unfortunately he now starts to weave a fantasy around Honor. As he describes his journey to Cambridge to announce his intense feelings for her, he sounds like a knight caught up in the tradition of courtly love: "The majesty . . . of these buildings seemed to add solemnity to my rite" (*SH*, 153). He envisions Honor as a maiden temporarily diverted by scholarly pursuits: "I . . . pictured the upstairs room as a study. Then I pictured her there sitting at a desk surrounded by books. Then I pictured myself beside her" (*SH*, 153–54). The repetition of the verb reinforces the solipsistic theme: some individuals do frequently act as if the existence of others depended upon a personal point of view. They do transform other real people into imaginary characters for their own private fantasies. As Martin breaks into Honor's home, he says, "My movements took on the quality of a dream. Things melted before me" (*SH*, 155). The errant knight is soon disillusioned when he finds his scholarly maiden in bed with her half-brother.

Murdoch may have various reasons for including this scene. One may be to point indirectly to the psychologically incestuous nature of many of the other relationships in the book: Antonia becomes Martin's mother; Georgie, his daughter; his brother Alexander looks like his father but embodies the spirit of his mother; and he dreams of his sister Rosemary. Another reason for the episode may be to show that Honor herself cannot be seen simply as a primitive Laurentian figure of positive de-

struction; she is after all an erudite professor and, as we now understand, suffers from her own special neurosis. The author is certainly also
satirizing psychiatry by making Palmer, the psychoanalyst, even more
deviant than his patients. Perhaps most of all Murdoch intends to shock
Martin out of his own solipsistic fantasies: clearly Honor is not there
waiting for him.

Martin does realize that his expectations of finding Honor virginal and
alone have been "obtuse," "naive," and "stupid" (*SH*, 156–57). He learns
this lesson quickly. But far from being deterred, he now seems even
more compelled, as he says, by that "tawny-breasted witch the vision of
whom . . . never ceased now to be before me" (*SH*, 167).

Honor also seems to have an unearthly influence upon Palmer, whose
darker side is now slowly revealed to Antonia. Martin's frightened wife
reports that Palmer like someone "possessed by the devil" frequently
stares at her as if he wants to kill her. She then tells Martin that "Honor
Klein has come back to the house and . . . seems to be everywhere at
once like a black cloud" (*SH*, 170).

Honor's hellish instruction of Martin continues as she makes Martin
feel the full weight of his responsibility for Georgie Hands, who indeed
has ceased to exist for Martin while he has been busy elsewhere. In
rebellion against being kept "in cold storage" for so long (*SH*, 181),
Georgie dallies with Martin's brother, cuts off her hair and sends it to
Martin, and finally tries to cut off her life by taking an overdose of pills.
As Honor and Martin kneel beside the unconscious Georgie, Honor like
an avenging fury casts her eyes upon Martin who says: "She was present
to me, but only as a torment, as an apparition; and I knew that I was
looking at her as I had never looked at any human being but as one
might look at a demon. . . . Then we both looked down at Georgie" (*SH*,
211).

In the festive recovery scene, where most of the other characters
happily chatter around Georgie's hospital bed, Martin feels Honor
Klein's penetrating stare: "it seemed to have become extremely difficult
to move or speak, as if I were being subjected to some paralyzing ray"
(*SH*, 216).

Besides calling attention to Martin's responsibility for Georgie's suicide
attempt, the passage also reinforces the Medusa image that had been
used earlier to describe Honor (*SH*, 188). While commenting on the
sculptured heads in his studio, Martin's brother Alexander recalls the
Freudian interpretation of Medusa, reminding Martin that the severed
head can represent "the female genitals, feared not desired" (*SH*, 50).
These references coalesce when Honor, reacting to Martin's obsession
with her, tells him she is only an object of "terrible fascination" for him:

I am a severed head as primitive tribes and old alchemists used to use, anointing it with oil and putting a morsel of gold upon its tongue to make it utter prophecies. And who knows but that long acquaintance with a severed head might not lead to strange knowledge. For such knowledge one would have paid enough. But that is remote from love and remote from ordinary life. As real people we do not exist for each other. (*SH*, 221)

Thus the book's title as well as Honor Klein resonates with multiple meanings to express the complexity of the relationship that develops between Martin and Honor. Honor does sever the mask of civilized hypocrisy worn by Antonia and Palmer, but in another sense she herself is the mysterious "severed head" used by primitive tribes. She certainly serves as a source of "strange knowledge" for Martin. And the Freudian Medusa interpretation also applies because in spite of his promiscuity, Martin is really frightened of women. Part of his attraction to Honor depends upon his being afraid of her: she is "dangerous" (*SH*, 86). Besides other implications, the sword scene can, of course, suggest his fear of castration. Although attracted to her, he hesitantly crosses his legs as he marvels at the awesome sword-wielding woman. He is tempted to take the sword, but "something prevented [him]" (*SH*, 118). Besides needing to crash through Palmer and Antonia's civilized construct, Martin needs to overcome his fear of women in general. He needs a woman who will be not his mother nor his daughter but his true mate.

Honor Klein thus wears various mythic and symbolic garments. But does a real woman lurk beneath all this dark apparel and will Martin be strong enough to overcome his neurosis and find out? Can Martin and Honor—contrary to her claim—"exist for each other as real people"?

Honor's comment about real people might make one wonder about the form of the entire novel. Do any of these people seem real in a book where the tragic and the comic, the serious and the silly are frequently juxtaposed as if Murdoch herself wanted to keep upsetting the reader's preconceptions about how he is supposed to react to particular aesthetic forms? After Martin summons enough courage to strike Palmer in the face, for instance, he soon finds himself asking his wife's lover for a few shillings to pay the furniture men, who themselves become a comic device as they indifferently lug Martin's furniture back and forth throughout the work as partners periodically change. One critic has labeled the novel a "Freudian nightmare treated in terms of drawing-room comedy."[5] Others have compared it to Restoration drama.

Certainly elements of satire and parody are strong. Suggesting a game of musical beds, the various couples pass through still another series of permutations so that we finally see Antonia and Alexander jaunting off to decadent Rome while Palmer Anderson and Georgie fly to America. Antonia seems especially puppet-like as she informs Martin of her second lover, his brother Alexander. Her earlier confession "about me and Anderson" becomes a hundred or so pages later an announcement "about me and Alexander," as each time she pours the rest of her drink into Martin's glass (*SH*, 25, 226). And the "solid structure" (*SH*, 32) of Martin's marriage to Antonia proves to be an illusion from the start because Antonia and Alexander had been lovers even before Martin's marriage. The solipsistic theme assumes additional ironies near the end of the novel as Martin asks Antonia, "You mean our marriage never really existed at all" (*SH*, 228)? But Antonia insists that she loves both brothers and still wants to keep Martin in her "loving net" (*SH*, 231).

As she moves on from Anderson to Alexander, reinforcing her "mystique" about men whose names begin with "A," Antonia speaks "softly, rubbing [Martin's] cheek as if she were rubbing into it some spellbinding ointment" (*SH*, 231). But because of Honor's demonic influence, Martin can now resist Antonia's fatuous attempts to enchant him once again by being hard and ironic from the outset. He glibly remarks to Antonia, "Well, it's nice that you won't have to change your name. It will be so much less confusing for the tradespeople. I'm glad we're keeping you in the family" (*SH*, 231). The repetitious imagery surrounding Antonia's announcements makes her relationships seem all the more mechanical and trivial, and she becomes for the reader as well as for Martin a grotesque caricature rather than a real person.

Georgie Hands shows a certain earthy integrity, but she is not really developed enough to become a strong central character. The test of the novel depends upon the relationship between Honor and Martin. As we have seen, Honor Klein is cloaked in symbolism and myth. The demonic metaphors break through the web of genteel fantasy that Antonia, Palmer, and even Martin himself have tangled about themselves throughout the novel. Just before Martin met Honor, for instance, he had complained of Antonia and Palmer's influence in terms of "a strangler's rope. . . . I was their prisoner and I choked with it. But I too much feared the darkness beyond" (*SH*, 62). The Nietzchean Honor Klein provides the searing force needed to cut through the "tender bond" (*SH*, 62) of this civilized cage. Ironically she also provides Martin with the "darkness" that allows him to "see." But does Honor herself emerge from her symbolic demonism and enter the real world?

The imagery suggests that she does. Although the demonic references continue to the end of the book implying that her primitive impulses will never nor should ever be completely submerged, the dark imagery is complemented by pervasive light in the final scenes of the novel suggesting a breakthrough more positive than the gray, gloomy ending of *The*

Flight from the Enchanter. Toward the end of the work Martin receives some hope from Honor's trembling hand and says, "When one is in love a little light shines a long way" (*SH*, 225). Soon Honor drives with Palmer to the airport but returns to Martin, who begins the last chapter of the novel with "I turned all the lights on" (*SH*, 242). As Honor stands outside in the "semi-darkness" Martin looks back and lets Honor follow him "in towards the light" (*SH*, 245). The pattern continues until the last sentence where he returns the "bright light" of her smile. The intense light imagery suggests that the two are finally "seeing" each other as real individuals rather than as mythological monsters or sweet darlings in a civilized fantasy. Unlike Mischa Fox, who enchanted in order to confuse and enslave, Honor Klein has used her dark power in order to clarify and liberate.

Having an apprehension of Honor "which is deeper than ordinary knowledge" (*SH*, 220), Martin has desperately tried to approach Honor as an equal. Realizing the destructive nature of her obsession with her brother, Honor has also come to Martin, anticipating the chance of freedom through the recognition of his otherness. Besides the intensified light imagery, the spinning pace of the novel suddenly slows down in this final chapter so that every word, every look, every gesture assumes great importance as two people perhaps for the first time perceive each other clearly. Martin exults: "An intoxicating sense possessed me that at last we were treating on equal terms. I kept my face stern, but there was so much light within, it must have showed a little" (*SH*, 247).

The title of the book thus applies to its form as well as to its content. Murdoch shows that she is not tyrannized by form: in the last chapter she severs the satiric mask of the rest of the novel. The mythic clothing of Honor Klein is also loosened. The tone becomes more naturalistic and no more puppet-like Antonias jangle about. Instead, two real people emerge. The demonic Honor Klein has done her didactic work and can now confront Martin as a real woman. The proof of Martin's growth lies in the ultimately perceptive narration he has just composed.

THE EVIL EYE
The Unicorn

After the dark surrealism of *A Severed Head,* Murdoch swings back to a more domestic everyday world in *An Unofficial Rose,* but in her seventh novel she attempts one of her boldest experiments in the literature of suspense and terror. In many ways *The Unicorn* epitomizes demonic didacticism in the fiction of Iris Murdoch.

An eerie atmosphere enshrouds the entire novel, which ranks as Murdoch's most Gothic work of literature to date—complete with a desolate seascape and dangerous bogs surrounding a mysterious castle with dark passageways where obsessed people are imprisoned, whipped, and murdered. Strangely, this explicitly terrifying novel becomes highly didactic because the Gothic form, macabre enough in itself, is also used for its allegorical implications. In fact, Murdoch's most Gothic novel turns out to be her most allegorical: many of the characters tend to represent ideas. We thus find some of the strengths and weaknesses of a novel where ideas can become more important than the characters themselves. But before critics protest that they are not interested in such an ideological work of fiction,[1] they should consider that the central moral lesson which Murdoch wants to convey involves the idea that we must not impose myths or theories upon other human beings, who must retain their unique qualities in a contingent world free of artificial patterns. As one character in the novel says, "No one should be a prisoner of other people's thoughts, no one's destiny should be an object of fascination to others."[2]

To illustrate her thesis Murdoch has created a myth or allegory about a number of people trapped within various versions of a legend. That some of these people do not seem quite realistic in one sense supports Murdoch's thesis: people do become mechanical and artificial when they succumb to the temptations of form and adhere to an externally imposed pattern. The novel proves to be a tour de force: in order to illustrate the evils of myth and fantasy Murdoch herself creates a fantastic myth. Humor, for instance, which frequently strays outside a formal pattern, seems conspicuously minimal in this stark novel by a writer for whom the comic plays such an important role in many of her other works. One might argue that this book expresses a tragic view of life. But so do *The Black Prince, A Fairly Honourable Defeat,* and *The Sacred and Profane Love Machine,* which also become very comic in many ways that this work does not. One does sense from time to time, however, that in *The Unicorn* Murdoch plays with the Gothic form itself, defiantly exploiting obvious techniques, perhaps to emphasize the greater significance of the ideas. One should at any rate certainly keep the allegorical element in mind upon entering the gloomy world of the novel.

At the center of the novel's legend quietly sits Hannah Crean-Smith, who for seven years has supposedly been locked up in a remote English castle by her cruel and dissipated husband, Peter Crean-Smith, who seven years earlier found his wife in bed with a young neighbor named Pip Lejour. Upon this discovery, a violent argument ensued in which Hannah somehow pushed her husband over the steep coastal cliff on the castle grounds. Miraculously Peter survived by landing on a ledge but was reputedly maimed for life. As punishment for her transgressions, which seem minor when compared to her husband's lustful indulgences, Hannah was restricted to the isolated estate "guarded" by Gerald Scottow, Peter's friend and henchman, who took command while Peter enjoyed himself in New York. Other "guardians" soon arrived in the form of Peter's poor relatives, Violet Evercreech and her younger brother Jamesie, who nominally assumed the positions of housekeeper and chauffeur. At the time of the fateful struggle a violent storm and flood had ravaged much of the landscape; consequently, the superstitious townspeople in the nearby small fishing village linked the eerie events at the castle with the wild storm and created a legend around Hannah Crean-Smith, who they believed would die if she ever left the dreary estate. They also predicted that after seven years—when the novel begins—there would be another cataclysmic turn of events.

Herein lies the central web of the myth around which more and more coils are woven as the story progresses. The reader knows nothing of this strange legend at the outset of the novel but must learn about it in bits and pieces through the eyes of the book's two main narrators from the "outside" world: Marian Taylor, a children's governess who discovers that at this unusual home there are no children; and Effingham Cooper, a civil servant who sometimes visits Pip Lejour's father, a philosopher who resides at Riders, the only other estate within miles of the legendary homestead significantly called Gaze Castle.

The name is well chosen because Murdoch's novel examines a group of people who speculate upon the events at the castle and then construct rigid networks of interpretation that ultimately imprison them as they act out their fantastic theories. As Rubin Rabinovitz has said, "To live according to a myth destroys contingency; if one is deluded by fantasies it is impossible to see, and to love, others."[3] Many of the individuals form relationships that become demonic in that one partner seems possessed by the other. Murdoch's didactic work demonstrates that true evil and demonic power really result from a failure of vision. Unique traits of individuals are not recognized when human beings become fixed objects in a mythic system. Everyone gazes at Hannah, but they do not look objectively: they see her only as a character in their private dramas—not as a real woman.

They gaze through the subjective filters of their fanciful minds and not with true awareness: they do not really "see" or attend to her unique otherness. Besides symbolically naming her Gothic mansion Gaze Castle, Murdoch indicates the importance of "seeing" others clearly through several additional motifs. Physical vision itself often becomes difficult in this treacherous landscape where several people get lost in the murky bogs. When Marian Taylor first looks at Riders in the "sunny mist" it had "something of the air of a mirage" (U, 10). Innumerable times she has trouble identifying the shadowy forms who pass through the poorly lit hallways of Gaze Castle where people are always "vanishing into the darkness" (U, 14). In the downstairs sitting room "the oil lamps, which she could not relight, went out" (U, 38).

Miss Taylor's new binoculars, which she first uses upon arriving at the castle, seem especially symbolic in that throughout the entire novel she, along with the reader, engages in a series of attempts to bring people and places into focus. When she first sees Jamesie Evercreech in the back of the dark car that picks her up at the railroad station, she initially perceives him as a big dog, then a shaggy fifteen-year-old boy, and finally, a young man of about nineteen. Even when she gets a better look, she has difficulty "placing" him: can he be her student or one of the servants? Later in the novel when she wanders into Jamesie's room, she has difficulty adjusting to the dim light before she finally focuses on what at first appears to be "curious patterned wallpaper" but in reality proves to be hundreds of photographs of Gerald Scottow, sometimes naked "and in some very strange postures indeed" (U, 146).

Murdoch really wants, of course, a clear moral vision. Recalling the incident with the field glasses in The Flight from the Enchanter, the first time that Marian looks at Riders through her binoculars she is suddenly startled to see a man on the distant estate looking straight back at her through his own pair of binoculars. In both scenes the author taps a profoundly unnerving experience: a watcher's sudden realization that he too is being watched. Both episodes seem to imply that looking at others can implicate the observer—a potential involvement that causes Marian

Taylor to panic. Throughout the novel several other characters use field glasses. In fact, at Gaze Castle a number of observers filter other people through the "magic circle" (*U*, 15) of their subjective binoculars and never really expect to be in any way accountable themselves. Frequently watchers "fix" someone in a static role that allows for no contingency and thus no real life. Jamesie's pornographic photographs of Gerald, just like Calvin Blick's photographs in *The Flight from the Enchanter,* also suggest the attempt to capture fluid reality in a fixed form.

Perhaps the most pervasive image hinting that the real sickness at Gaze Castle results from a problem in perspective can be found in the mirror, which can imply subjectivity but also a failure to see beyond oneself to the reality of others. As in the dressing room scene in the *Enchanter,* here too Murdoch suggests that illusion and fantasy lie just beyond the looking glass. Hired as a lady's companion, Marian watches her ethereal mistress "glide about the room" moving "from glass to glass" and soon realizes that Hannah is "much given to looking at herself in mirrors" (*U*, 44). Hannah's fascination with the looking glass signifies the neurotic self-absorption that, as Murdoch has explained in several of her essays, can cultivate a paralysis of will. Marian keeps wondering why Hannah can not escape from Gaze Castle if she really wants to. Is Hannah too absorbed in her own sense of sin and suffering? Is the sleeping beauty imprisoned in a role she herself has refined? The palindrome in her very name symbolizes self-containment: Hannah also gazes at Hannah. At Riders, Effingham Cooper suspects that Max Lejour, a "prisoner of books, age, and ill health" who constantly thinks of Hannah, "might derive consolation from the spectacle, over there in the other house, of another captivity, a distorted mirror image of his own" (*U*, 105). In still another section, Cooper, who suddenly sees Max's daughter Alice in a new light, says, "It's as if I'd been, all the time, looking into a mirror, and only been vaguely conscious of the real world at my side" (*U*, 236). Dark hallways, binoculars, photographs, and mirrors all suggest that the demonic enchantment of Gaze Castle largely results from a distortion of vision.

At one point Marian thinks "Reactions at Gaze were slow and clouded" (*U*, 34). Indeed, besides the murkiness a sense of stagnation envelops the castle, with its "sleepy dragging routine" and its quietness that is "aimless rather than calm" (*U*, 28). Murdoch's Gothic setting then not only is gloomy in itself but also reinforces her didactic theme. Failure to recognize the reality of others leads to a static situation that can resemble death. As Marian looks out on the barren seascape, Gerald Scottow tells her "the place was killed by a big storm some years ago. . . . It's an empty land. . . . I doubt that there's a single tree between here and Greytown"

(*U*, 5, 6). She soon learns that the "inky black" ocean slopes off treacherously and swimming is not recommended in this "sea that kills" (*U*, 31, 8).

People trapped within demonic relationships are in many ways dead, and inside Gaze Castle the locks, keys, bolted doors, and other entrapment images reinforce Murdoch's thesis about the ultimately deadening effect of artificial structures imposed upon formless reality. The glass doors locking up all the books in the castle's sitting room provide the perfect symbol of the barriers that have been erected against new outlooks and knowledge. And the entire entrapment motif is formally introduced by Hannah Crean-Smith's apparently innocuous first words to her new lady companion: "How wonderfully good of you to come. . . I do hope you won't mind being imprisoned with us here miles from anywhere" (*U*, 21).

"Prison" aptly describes a demonic relationship although the iron bars are manufactured in the foundry of the mind. Interestingly, Peter Crean-Smith, supposedly the real culprit in the imprisonment legend, is discussed by others but Marian never actually sees him until the end of the novel after he has died and has been wrapped in a sheet. Never seen as a real man, Smith nicely illustrates the demonic personality whose dark powers largely depend upon the fantasies of others.

In an interview with W. K. Rose, Iris Murdoch discussed

the notion of the intrusion of demons—well, I feel this is something that happens in life. Not necessarily that people really are demons but that they play the role of demons for other people. . . . I think there is a great deal of spare energy racing around, which very often— whether it comes from the unconscious mind or however one likes to describe this—suddenly focuses a situation and makes a person play a commanding role. People are often looking for a god or ready to cast somebody in the role of a demon . . . I think people possessed of this kind of energy do come in and generate situations. One's seen it happening in life. But then too there are always victims ready to come forward.[4]

A much more visible example of a demonic personality than Peter Crean-Smith, Gerald Scottow illustrates these ideas. But before he becomes a demonic master, Scottow acts as a type of slave to Peter Crean-Smith; he thus exemplifies Simone Weil's idea that the afflicted usually pass their suffering on to someone else. A sturdy local boy, Scottow works on Peter's estate and, according to Pip Lejour, the two become "obsessed with each other," engaging in a type of sexual feudalism in which Gerald plays the role of Peter's serf and even enjoys "being kicked around a bit" (*U*, 121). After the wild storm, Scottow serves as Hannah's jailer for Peter and gradually assumes Peter's traits. As one character later says, "Gerald is Peter now. He has Peter's place, he even looks like Peter" (*U*, 259).

After the suspenseful episode of Marian and Effingham's abortive attempt to free Hannah, Gerald Scottow comes to his "Maid Marian's" room for a little talk. Gerald's sexual magnetism becomes so compelling that Marian later realizes that Gerald could have had anything he wanted in that dark bedroom. During this encounter Scottow gives his theory of the demonic spell enveloping Gaze Castle:

> Happiness is a weak and paltry thing, and perhaps "freedom" has no meaning. There are great patterns in which we all are involved, and destinies which belong to us and which we love even in the moment when they destroy us. Do you think that I myself am separated in any way from what goes on here, that I am free? I am part of it too. It does not belong to me, I belong to it. And that is the only way it can be here, because of the pattern that is what has authority here, an absolute authority. And that is what anyone must submit to, if they are to stay here. (*U*, 168–69)

Gaze Castle contains a number of "victims," as Murdoch has described them in her interview; they submit to the demonic authority of Gerald Scottow, who decidedly "play[s] a commanding role." Scottow has certainly enthralled Jamesie Evercreech, who several years earlier also tried to free Hannah from the "great patterns" at Gaze Castle. After Gerald caught Jamesie packing Hannah's suitcase, he took Jamesie out to the stables and whipped him severely. After that, Jamesie worshipped and belonged to Gerald. The two men are now frequently seen as a pair: Jamesie hunched over before the taller Gerald or the younger man fawning by Gerald's polished boots as Gerald sits on a horse and touches Jamesie's cheek with his riding crop. These bizarre tableaus emphasize the static nature of the relationship. In several outdoor scenes Jamesie, a shy young man, begins to open up to Marian but immediately withdraws as Gerald approaches. One sad sentence succinctly expresses Gerald's dark influence, especially strong within the confines of the castle: "The house was very silent as [Marian] came in with Jamesie, and after they crossed the threshold his chatter at once subsided and he faded away into the shadow of the stairs" (*U*, 165).

When later in the novel a message arrives that Peter is returning, Hannah, more distraught than ever, also gives herself completely to Gerald. The two stay together for hours in Hannah's locked room. Marian at first thinks that Gerald "was there" when Hannah needed someone, but when another message reports that Peter cannot really return, Marian suspects the original cable to be fake—a forged letter perhaps even sent by Gerald himself. She feels that with his sexual conquest of Hannah, Gerald's domination becomes absolute: he has "with one quick twist, as of one manipulating a whirling rope, bound her, enslaved her, a thousand times more: and then proposed that the situation should continue . . ." (*U*, 246).

Murdoch handles her characterization of Gerald Scottow skillfully. Early in the novel through Marian's eyes Murdoch captures the ambivalence in Gerald's manner, "both solicitous and authoritative" (*U*, 36), and then one watches as the "reassuring grip" (*U*, 4) slowly tightens to a stranglehold. Although frequently seen in demonic shadows, Scottow can also be observed in a more realistic light. Pip Lejour calculates, for instance, that Gerald "works" at the castle because he had been a poor man whom Smith now pays "very handsomely" and who now often vacations all over the world on his mysterious periodic departures from Gaze. But even though his motives may be more mundane than many imagine, Gerald Scottow is still inextricably ensnared in the myth of Gaze Castle and remains for a number of the characters "the center from which the furies came" (*U*, 152).

At times Violet Evercreech personifies one of these furies. Like a phantom haunting Gaze Castle, Violet often frightens Marian Taylor by her unsettling habit of creeping up from behind. Marian senses that she is being watched closely by Violet and when talking to her feels "the degree of attention almost unendurable" (*U*, 20). Because of the stifling intensity she feels in Violet's presence and because of the sexual advances Violet makes one day, Marian suspects that the relationship between Violet and Hannah involves more than that between housekeeper and mistress. Violet often seems to be in charge of Hannah herself rather than her house. During the scene when Hannah breaks out in hysterical wailing when her attendant Denis Nolan sings, Violet commands Hannah to "Get up" and then leads her to her room as she would a naughty child.

We never really hear Violet's whole story although Marian wonders out of what love, hate, or fantasy Violet had approached her (*U*, 153). But we do learn that Violet, a poor relative, is very much interested in Hannah's fortune. An early episode in which she pockets the coin from a brass donkey while looking for a key to the bookcase foreshadows her obsession with money. Since Violet's interest in Gaze Castle seems the most materialistic and base, her "theory" about Hannah appropriately proves the most negative: during violent events near the novel's end, she calls Hannah a "murderess and whore" (*U*, 212). And when she learns that Hannah left her estate to Max Lejour, she screams "what a perfect bitch!" (*U*, 292). In the sinister portrait of Violet Evercreech, Murdoch makes the didactic point that obsession with money can turn people into evil forces.

The religious theories about Hannah Crean-Smith perhaps tend to be even more complicated and coercive. After discussing the demonic relationships in several of her other novels including *The Flight from the Enchanter* and *A Severed Head,* Murdoch commented in an interview that *The Unicorn* is about "the ambiguity of these kinds of strange relationships when they get mixed up with the spiritual world and with notions of redemption and with religious notions. In a way it is about the ambiguity of the spiritual world itself, about the curious connexions there are between spirituality and sex."[5] Murdoch's characterization of Hannah's devoted attendant Denis Nolan exemplifies this ambiguity.

Nolan's opening conversation with Gerald Scottow, in which he grunts and makes a few grudging monosyllabic replies, clearly shows that, unlike Jamesie, Denis pays homage to other gods (*U*, 20). Marian soon learns that Denis's theory about Hannah depends upon the Christian myth of salvation through redemption: he tells Marian that Hannah "has found over these last years a great and deep peace of mind. As I think, she has made peace with her God. . . . Her peace is her own and it is her best possession, whatever you believe" (*U*, 68).

Denis's religious notions do coalesce with sexual impulses. Besides the Christian God, Denis also worships Hannah. Pehaps in an effort to make her "peace" as tranquil as possible, he submits to her in an almost masochistic way when he serves as "her page." In the scene after he has cut her hair, she fondles him erotically as he "grovels at her feet" cleaning up her fallen locks. After he fetches her stockings, "he knelt again to put on her shoes" (*U*, 42).

In spite of his unusual devotion, Denis remains one of the few residents of Gaze Castle who is associated with nature and primitive vitality. Murdoch sees the natural world as a positive, spontaneous force that has the potential to pull Denis away from deterministic theories of sin and guilt. Like one of Lawrence's dark shaggy servants, Denis cares for the horses on the estate, frolics wildly with the dog, protects the goldfish from cranes, and brings Hannah wild pets such as hedgehogs and crippled bats. But even though he seems at home in its vitality, he tries to impose his Christian viewpoint upon the natural world. Discussing the salmon who struggle back to the spawning pool, he comments that all God's creatures must suffer. He undoubtedly sees Hannah as one of these creatures but tries to alleviate her suffering. Describing Hannah's plight for Marian, he says: "The soul under the burden of sin cannot flee. What is enacted here with her is enacted with all of us in one way or another. You cannot come between her and her suffering, it is too complicated" (*U*, 68).

Denis's theory about Hannah is complicated by his view of Peter Crean-Smith. His love for Hannah is stained by his intense hatred for Peter, who he feels has made Hannah's share of suffering greater than normal. It is Denis who sketches in for Marian most of the details of the imprisonment legend, becoming especially scathing in his remarks about Peter. Obsessed with his hatred of this man, Denis finally resolves to "fight evil with evil" (*U*, 260). Nolan's evil is realized in his responsibility for Peter's drowning on his final return to Gaze Castle. Marian intuits the demonic hatred overwhelming Denis when she thinks: "Denis and Peter were coming together. Now their figures merged strangely in her mind" (*U*, 284).

When he learns that Hannah has taken her life while he was dealing with Peter, Denis realizes that his obsession with Peter probably led to Hannah's death, for he feels that she would never have killed herself had he remained at her side. He confesses to Marian: "I did not only love, I also hated. And hatred can corrupt the love that makes it be. That was why I was not there when I should have been" (*U*, 301). Suggesting that the mythic cycle of sin and expiation will begin again, Denis assumes Hannah's guilt as Marian accordingly says, "Yes, you are becoming Hannah now" (*U*, 303). We last see Denis as he tramps off into the hills carrying his pet goldfish and his new burden of guilt.

Although Max Lejour lectures about the dangers of transforming Hannah into a Christian myth, urging that she must be seen "as real," he also neglects her reality and instead turns her into an object of philosophical contemplation. Frequently he equates her with Platonic conceptions of beauty and goodness, finding her story beautiful, "and because beauty is a spiritual thing it commands worship rather than arousing desire" (*U*, 106). He associates Hannah's quiet acknowledgment of unverified guilt with the Greek concept of Até, "which is the name of the almost automatic transfer of suffering from one being to another. Power is a form of Até. . . . But Good is non-powerful. And it is in the good that Até is finally quenched, when it encounters a pure being who only suffers and does not attempt to pass the suffering on." But when Effingham asks if Hannah can be considered such a pure being, Max, keeping true to the speculative nature of philosophy, replies that he remains unsure: "She may be just a sort of enchantress, a Circe, a spiritual Penelope keeping her suitors spellbound and enslaved" (*U*, 107). Although Max Lejour is highly perceptive, he never acts upon his insights, making "Riders" the name of his estate seem somewhat ironic. Discussing Hannah's story, he says, "It has all seemed to me so delicate that any action would be too gross" (*U*, 104). Afraid of being disturbed in his scholarly pursuits, Max has never visited Hannah during her long confinement. Like Marcus Fisher in *The Time of the Angels* and Rupert Foster in *A Fairly Honourable Defeat*, both of whom labor on monumental works of ethics, Max Lejour proves to be another one of Murdoch's great theoreticians who pale at the thought of a practical application of their lofty ideals. Lejour's aloof position within range of someone he describes as "our image of the significance of suffering" seems somewhat spectral. Although Murdoch's characterization of Max Lejour could be thought weak in that he often appears to represent only a mouthpiece for her philosophical musings, perhaps this apparent aesthetic flaw again represents one of Murdoch's lessons: theoreticians who seldom act do in one sense lack substance.

Before examining how the two outside narrators find their way through the maze of ideas surrounding Gaze Castle, we might profit by first taking a closer look at Hannah, who plays a crucial role in the legend. Murdoch's powers of characterization are especially challenged here because she must create a personality shadowy enough to permit at least the possibility of the multiple theories enveloping Hannah. Murdoch achieves this task by painting an ethereal, dream-like figure who wears flowing yellow nightgowns and is often surrounded by golden light suggesting illusion. Several different characters see Hannah as "beautiful and spiritual-looking in a rather fey way" (*U*, 25) or as "marvellously strange . . . a fey, almost demonic creature sometimes" with a "cutlooseness from ordinary being" (*U*, 100). Her personality also remains sufficiently ambivalent to allow for various evaluations. At times she appears to be a passive victim: her seven-year-old shoes that look brand-new attest to her incarceration; she gulps down whiskey as a form of escape; and after the frustrated rescue she is led back to the castle "like a sleepwalker" by Gerald Scottow (*U*, 163). Other times she seems less innocent as when she remarks about Denis Nolan, "I think he would let me kill him slowly" (*U*, 44) or as when later in the novel she actually uses a gun.

The ambivalence in Hannah Crean-Smith's character is reinforced by the symbol that serves as the book's title. Effingham Cooper first calls Hannah a "legendary creature, a beautiful unicorn" (*U*, 106). But Max Lejour reminds him that in medieval mythology "the unicorn is also the image of Christ" and thus Hannah can be thought of as a suffering Christ figure as well. Robert Scholes has pointed out that Hannah's last name, Crean-Smith, can be seen as an anagram for Christ-mean or Christ-name, but feels that the palindrome in her first name indicates an ambiguity in Hannah's position that "works to undercut and make relative the Christian view of the cosmos."[6] Thus the unicorn, like the severed head, accrues multiple meanings to incorporate the complexity of the character it signifies. Accordingly in *Psychology and Alchemy* Carl Jung writes that "the unicorn is not a single, clearly defined entity but a fabulous being with a great many variations."[7] After acknowledging the associations with Christ, Jung remarks that the unicorn also "harbours in itself an inner contradiction." St. Basil warns that the unicorn "is the

Demon. For he plotteth evil against man."[8] And in Judaic mythology the unicorn has become "a personification of the daemonic forces of nature."[9] Suggesting both the devil and Christ, the unicorn, like Hannah herself, embodies both the demonic and didactic impulses of this novel.

Indeed, Hannah's last comments to the other characters form a parable shaded in spectral images:

> It was your belief in the significance of my suffering that kept me going. Ah, how much I needed you all! I have battened upon you like a secret vampire. . . . I needed my audience, I lived in your gaze like a false God. But it is the punishment of a false God to become unreal. . . . You have made me unreal by thinking about me so much. You made me into an object of contemplation. (U, 249)

When the terrible news arrives that Peter Crean-Smith will return to Gaze Castle, Hannah finally breaks out of the mythic patterns that have enveloped her, but like the storm that floods the surrounding valley, contingent reality rushes in so forcefully that it produces chaos, violence, and death.

But what do the two observers from the civilized urban world make of all this madness and disaster? Since both Marian Taylor and Effingham Cooper are highly educated, one might expect their sophisticated modern minds to be able to sift through the wreckage in order to separate fact from fantasy. One might even hope for a selfless attention that could pierce the mythic clouds surrounding Gaze Castle and focus on the real woman inside. But unfortunately Murdoch suggests that demonic enchantment is in no way limited to the inhabitants of the moors.

Although Marian Taylor equipped with binoculars certainly makes a commendable effort to see clearly, she is handicapped by a tendency to filter life through Romantic lenses. After accepting the position at Gaze Castle, for instance, she does not announce the exact time of her arrival since, as she says, "It had seemed more exciting, more romantic and somehow less alarming to come at her own pace" (U, 3). While being escorted to the castle by Gerald and Jamesie, Marian reacts in a highly emotional manner described in breathless staccato prose:

> Marian was suddenly overcome by an appalling, crippling panic. She was very frightened at the idea of arriving. But it was more than that. She feared the rocks and the cliffs and the grotesque dolmen and the ancient secret things. Her two companions seemed no longer reassuring but dreadfully alien and even sinister. She felt, for the first time in her life, completely isolated and in danger. She became in an instant almost faint with terror.[10]

Her new situation in a strange land could account for her emotionalism, but as several perceptive readers have noticed, the novel's language could in places easily describe a nineteenth-century sentimental heroine like Jane Eyre. Phrases such as "appalling, crippling panic," "dreadfully alien and even sinister," "completely isolated and in danger," and "almost faint with terror" give a melodramatic coloration to her experience.

Marian's tendency to dramatize life seems to reinforce her Romantic outlook. Recovering from an unsuccessful relationship with someone called Geoffrey, she now seems ready for some greater drama: "She was very nearly thirty; and her sense of life hitherto as a series of makeshift stage setting preliminaries had made her the more rapaciously welcoming to what seemed at last an event" (U, 6). Theater imagery continues to permeate her thought: trying on Hannah's jewelry, "Marian felt as if she and Hannah were on a stage, so violent and unusual was the lighting" (U, 51); and when Violet makes seductive gestures, Marian "hoped there would be no sequel; yet she had not wholly, not altogether, disliked it, the drama, the sheer unexpectedness" (U, 145). She soon begins to sense the larger drama involving Hannah and anticipates Gerald's remarks about "great patterns" when she thinks the events at Gaze Castle form "a tale in which nothing happened at random" (U, 67). She fluctuates, however, in her degree of participation in the "plot." As she learns more about the darker side of Gerald Scottow, she perceives her role as "his adversary, his opposite angel. By wrestling with Scottow she would make her way into the story" (U, 67). However, at other times she hints at an ultimate lack of involvement when she sees herself as a member of the audience rather than as one of the players. After her adventure with Denis Nolan in the salmon pool, she walks back to the castle: "With the return to Gaze she felt again her connection with the house and with the drama it had contained. But she felt towards it rather as one who is leaving a theatre after some tragic play, worn, torn, yet rejoiced and set free with a new appetite for the difficult world" (U, 232).

Besides her tendency to see life as a drama, Marian's modern liberal philosophy reinforces her Romanticism. Her description of the liberating effect of her intimate encounter with Denis Nolan even becomes somewhat tendentious: "This was freedom, the freedom to love and move which she had so terribly lacked" (U, 229). Or later we read, "I am free, thought Marian, as she watched [Denis] out of the room, we are free" (U, 237). Similarly, her prescription for Hannah's malaise is colored by liberal terminology and an existential emphasis upon individual responsibility and personal choice:

And now [Hannah] is simply spellbound. She's psychologically paralyzed. She's lost her sense of freedom. . . . Give her a shock. Pull her out of it just far enough to make her realize that she is free and that she's got to make her own decisions. (U, 130)

Marian's kidnapping scheme itself proves to be a somewhat Romantic notion. She has little idea of what she and Effingham will do with Hannah once they whisk her away from Gaze Castle; she only thinks: "Soon we shall leave them all behind, soon we shall be off on the road together, Hannah and Effingham and I. . . . What her own role would later on be she did not pause to consider. Her thought ended with the breaking of the barrier" (*U*, 157, 159).

At this stage in her thinking Murdoch believed love and truth to be more important than freedom and assertion of individual will, and her response to Marian's modern liberal attitudes is suggested in Max Lejour's comment: "That rag freedom! Freedom may be a value in politics but it's not a value in morals. Truth, yes. But not freedom. That's a flimsy idea, like happiness. In morals, we are all prisoners, but the name of our cure is not freedom" (*U*, 105). Additional comments upon Marian's philosophy of freedom are found not only in the failure of her rescue attempt but also in the grim fact that when Marian finally releases Hannah from her locked bedroom, Hannah uses that "freedom" to jump off a cliff and kill herself.

Even though Marian suffers from problems in perspective shared by the other characters, she does grow. That she will in any way be a receptive student to the terrible lessons of Gaze becomes understandable in that Marian is herself a teacher, "whose desire to instruct was always considerable" (*U*, 28) and who has always been interested in both ends of the educational process. Happy to fill dragging hours by agreeing to read poetry to Hannah, Marian "was glad too in quite a simple way of the prospect of once again instructing . . . There was no doubt that she was the little pedagogue" (*U*, 38). But Murdoch shows that Marian herself like Martin Lynch-Gibbon has a great lesson to learn about the reality of other human beings. Her potential for learning is indicated when she receives Greek lessons from Effingham Cooper, who finds Marian a "delightful and intelligent pupil" with a "hard, lively mind eager for instruction" (*U*, 124).

But Effingham teaches her only Greek grammar. Marian is not provided with a guide like Honor Klein, who used her dark powers for moral instruction. Most of the demonic powers in this novel flow into destructive channels. Handicapped by her Romantic outlook, Marian must therefore stumble through the gothic landscape on her own before she can finally come to a more realistic appraisal of life and other human beings. But this bizarre new world begins to be a source of education.

She is profoundly disturbed, for instance, by the tragic events at Gaze and especially by the part she might have played in Hannah's death. The framework of her liberal philosophy suddenly creaks: "had she done right to give Hannah this last thing, the freedom to make her life over in her own way into her own property? When at last Hannah had wanted to break the mirror, to go out through the gate, ought she then to have been her jailer? It was not any more the old images of freedom which could move her now" (*U*, 283).

As a result of her devastating experience, however, Marian Taylor begins to see things more clearly. After Hannah has shot Gerald Scottow, Marian even appraises Gerald's dead body with a new objectivity: no matter what demonic role he previously played, "now in the black middle of the night it was the fact of death that mattered most, the translation of a big healthy, powerful man into a piece of senseless stuff" (*U*, 276). She also comes to realize that she cannot incorporate Denis Nolan into her private drama but instead recognizes his otherness as he walks off into the hills with his new burden. Through the more positive aspects of both Marian's and Denis's characters, Murdoch suggests that one might alleviate the neurosis in human relationships not through abstract theories of religion and philosophy but through a direct and steady awareness of the reality of others, which is sometimes called love.

If the demonic events at Gaze Castle begin to teach Marian Taylor certain ethical truths, Effingham Cooper stiffly resists all moral education. Making his recalcitrance somewhat ironic, Cooper gives Marian Greek lessons and finds "himself suddenly nostalgic for the days when he had been a teacher. There was something singularly purifying in the business of teaching" (*U*, 124). A few Greek lessons notwithstanding, Cooper himself can no longer be considered a teacher. Nor does he prove to be a very good pupil. The respect he once felt for his former mentor Max Lejour has certainly faded: "One could not go on regarding one's old tutor as an infallible source of wisdom" (*U*, 308).

Using the ubiquitous mirror image, Murdoch's opening description of her civil servant suggests the weaknesses that make him a poor student:

> Effingham Cooper gazed out of the window of his first-class railway carriage. The landscape was just beginning to be familiar. Now each scene told him what was coming next. It was a moment that always affected him with pleasure and fear. There was the round tower, there was the ruined Georgian house with the dentil cornice, there was the big leaning megalith, there at last were the yellowish-grey rocks which marked the beginning of the Scarren. Although there was still another twenty minutes to go he took down his suitcases, put on his coat, and straightened his tie, regarding himself gravely in the carriage mirror. (*U*, 73)

Giving a clue to his essential egotism, the paragraph begins and ends with Effingham Cooper. He gazes at himself in the mirror more seriously than at the scenery outside the window, which also becomes a type of looking glass for his memory. Afraid of any change in the landscape, he quickly reassures himself that the outdoor sights coincide with the images he has fixed in his mind: "each scene told him what was coming next." The style of the prose in this passage also suggests Cooper's fear of change and his obsessive need for fixity. The lack of vital verbs and the repetition of the dull being verb in the sentences describing the landscape point to Effingham's lifeless outlook. In the fifth sentence the parallel series of simple clauses with expletives routinely noting the various landmarks as so many items on a list also implies Effingham's tendency to impose rigid structures upon fluid reality. Even in the sixth sentence the parallelism as well as the meaning of the three verb phrases reinforces a mechanical sense of habit. Effingham "took . . . put . . . and straightened": nothing must be out of place—in the landscape or on himself. His only three actions lead nowhere except back to Effingham, no longer regarding the scenery but only his own image in the mirror. For Effingham the two types of "gazing" are really the same: he imposes his preconceptions onto the shifting landscape. After all of his "outward" looking to what Marian saw as awesome terrain, Effingham Cooper, settled in his first-class compartment, routinely concludes, "It was a hot day."

After such a passage one wonders if the name Cooper could be an ironic counterpart for the American novelist who wrote so vividly about great explorations in a wild land. We soon learn that Murdoch's Cooper looks at people just as he looks at the landscape. He wants to stake out human relationships in the same way that he maps out the moors. Although six months have passed since he last visited his friends, he reassures himself, "he would find them unchanged. Doubtless they would find him unchanged" (*U*, 73). When he calls on Hannah, he again starts making lists: "Everything was blessedly the same: the whisky bottle, the mess of papers, the little sleepy fire, the pampas grass." The phrase "Everything was the same" is repeated three times within several pages (*U*, 95–97). After a few days back at the moors, Effingham, in fact, finds the whole situation "had taken on a certain settled form. Hannah was glad to see him, the Lejours were glad to see him; he had his place" (*U*, 80).

For Effingham "place" becomes synonymous with ego: he asserts himself by imposing structures upon his surroundings, but the framework becomes so rigid that life is destroyed. Murdoch emphasizes this point when one night Effingham suddenly loses his "place" when he wanders into the bogs. Here he finds "no sign indeed of anything now which could serve as a landmark" (*U*, 180). As he gropes about in the strange dark environment, the thought of evil as a positive force terrifies Effingham so that "he began to wish that he had a crucifix with him" (*U*, 185).

No vampires assail Effingham, but as he sinks deeper into the quick-sand, he is assaulted by stark realization that he will soon die. But with this grim awareness comes an illuminating vision. He suddenly understands that only by transcending the ego can one truly see and love what exists outside oneself:

> Since he was mortal he was nothing, and since he was nothing all that was not himself was filled to the brim with being, and it was from this that the light streamed. This then was love, to look and look until one exists no more, this was the love which was the same as death. He looked and knew, with a clarity which was one with the increasing light, that with the death of the self the world becomes quite automatically the object of a perfect love. (*U*, 189)

Perhaps in an effort to avoid being too allegorical, Murdoch often allows some of her most profound thoughts to pass through the mind of a character who seems least able to understand or act upon them. Unlike Marian Taylor, for instance, Cooper never overcomes "his distaste for the fascinating notion of using field glasses" (*U*, 77), suggesting that he does not even want to try to improve his outlook. And indeed after he is "saved" by Denis Nolan and led back to Gaze Castle, his momentary insight soon blurs. Glowing with the medicinal whiskey Hannah, Marian, and Alice have been pouring down his throat, Effingham "tried to focus his gaze upon the women, but they drew together into a single fuzzy golden orb" (*U*, 193). His subsequent actions and thoughts demonstrate that he loses the meaning of the moral lesson experienced on the moors but soon recovers his "monumental ego" (*U*, 309).

Murdoch shows that in spite of his culture, gentility, and rare visionary moments, Effingham Cooper must be considered just as guilty as some of the more brutish jailers keeping Hannah Crean-Smith locked up in Gaze Castle. Cooper spins his imagery around Hannah even while he works in the city where he reflects that the Gaze legend "had undeniably the qualities of a wonderful story. And as he sat in his office, dreaming of Hannah, he found himself feeling a certain strange guilty pleasure at the idea that she was, somehow, for him shut up, reserved, sequestered" (*U*, 80).

Effingham turns the strange incidents at Gaze into a lovely medieval legend with Hannah as the beautiful princess locked up in the tower and himself as a knight enthralled in the ritual of courtly love: "the odd spiritual, tormented yet resigned beauty of Hannah seemed to him now the castle perilous toward which he had all his days been faring" (*U*, 78). He even kneels before "his imprisoned lady" (*U*, 125) during one of their reunions. Of course, alterations in the medieval landscape also upset Effingham. For instance, he always finds the first encounter between the mythic and the actual woman a bit "alarming" (*U*, 88) as he realizes the large part his imagination has played in forming the ideal. Even though Effingham promises to help Marian "rescue" Hannah, at other times "thoughts of taking her away suddenly seemed unbearably crude" (*U*, 100).

Similarly, Effingham never offers physical love to his "princess," a restraint that probably explains why Gerald Scottow tolerates his visits. Eventually Cooper even analyzes his abstract love for Hannah in terms of Freudian psychology: "because of his unconscious resentment of his own mother's sin of sex, he had been, he explained, unable to establish any satisfactory relations with women other than those of Courtly Love. He would identify the woman he loved with his mother and then make her unapproachable and holy . . ." (*U*, 267). Whether it be the moors, his medieval landscape, or erotic zones, Effingham Cooper refuses to become an explorer.

Cooper's sexual problems aside, Murdoch suggests that his imprisonment of Hannah in his medieval fantasy is as cruel as her incarceration by others whose motives may not be so psychologically intriguing. In subtle ways Murdoch shows similarities between the refined civil servant and the other, more obviously demonic personalities. While Gerald Scottow dominates his band of followers, Effingham Cooper muses, "The idea of every woman after him was not displeasing" (*U*, 82). Indeed, in the course of the novel he believes that no fewer than five of the female characters are romantically interested in him, including the maid at Riders. Only several pages after Marian trembles at the demonic power of Gerald Scottow, who could have had "anything he wished" of her in that dark bedroom (*U*, 173), we find Effingham Cooper assuming that the maid loves him "and would do anything that he wished" (*U*, 178). Although the contrast becomes ironic, Murdoch implies that the polite residents from the "real world" can be as ruthless as the denizens of the Gothic environment of Gaze Castle. Cooper certainly seems callous with Alice Lejour whom for years he has "entangled . . . in a profitless love" (*U*, 75), while to him she has remained only an "incident" in the larger story concerning Hannah (*U*, 307). His participation in that larger story makes him as culpable as anyone else when Jamesie Evercreech says, "The play is over, the Vampire Play, let us call it. The blood is all shed that we used to drink" (*U*, 292).

While Cooper is disturbed by the bloody pheasants and guns carried by Gerald Scottow and his hunting friends, he himself tracks down Pip Lejour as "his quarry" when he wants some information about the Gaze legend (*U*, 114). Elsewhere he thinks of Pip as a butterfly he wants to net: "it was about time, in any case, for the elusive, fluttering, mocking Pip to be cornered, pinned down, and somehow accounted for" (*U*, 113). While Effingham seems shocked when Pip talks about certain fish who eat their mates, he himself says about Hannah, "We are all eating her up some-how, all of us" (*U*, 156–57). Cannibalism is also lightly suggested at the novel's end: when leaving Gaze on his train, Effingham Cooper settles down with the newspapers for a little "repast of triviality" that turns out to be an account of Pip Lejour's suicide (*U*, 310). One is reminded here of the submerged cannibalism of Huxley's "Nuns at Luncheon" and the final dinner scene in Joyce's "A Painful Case"—also involving a news-paper account.

Appropriately Effingham Cooper reads about the last death in *The Unicorn* because for him all the tragic events at Gaze Castle have simply amounted to chapters in a story. He had always appreciated Max Le-jour's interest in Hannah but did not want the philosopher invading his fictional world: "his enjoyment depended upon his retaining his own expertise, depended upon its remaining precisely a story" (*U*, 113). The form of the story rather than its meaning really interests Effingham. His habit of imposing structures upon various physical and psychological "places" manifests his obsessive need for form which he uses to assert his ego.

This aesthetic process becomes especially evident on the train which provides Cooper with an unnecessary physical distance from the violent events at Gaze Castle. In recalling Hannah, Effingham thinks, "The memory was smooth and rounded like a piece of amber. It smelled of an old degenerate happiness. He had been glad to have her reserved, sequestered, caged" (*U*, 309). For Effingham even Pip's death "rounded the thing off, gave it a tragic completeness which made it all the easier to cut free of it, to let it drift away like a great buoyant sphere into the past" (*U*, 310). Through his aesthetic distance Effingham Cooper transforms the murderous violence of Gaze Castle into smooth pieces of amber and buoyant spheres. Suggesting that he never really got off the train, Cooper is settled once again in his first-class compartment. His ability to impose a pretty crystalline shape upon tragic contingency allows him to ride away from the bloodshed of Gaze thinking: "It had been a curious and not unpleasant interval with a sense of holiday about it" (*U*, 306). Murdoch makes the moral point that such aesthetic formulation is truly demonic.

Her idea here may even explain why—after the formalist preoccupa-tion with complex symbolic structures used to project a solipsistic vi-sion—she herself employs techniques that become unabashedly didactic. The politely demonic Effingham Cooper can represent the modern artist so obsessed with form that he loses sight of real moral value.

PART II

Muriel Spark

THE INTRUDER
The Ballad of Peckham Rye

About the same time that Iris Murdoch was beginning her prolific career, another British woman started writing fiction but in a somewhat different form. The sardonic novels of Muriel Spark tend to be shorter and more compact than those of Iris Murdoch, whose prose can become more expansive. Spark writes a deceptively simple yet elegant prose that often recalls the rhythms and pristine clarity of the nursery rhyme. In spite of stylistic differences, however, both authors have searched for moral themes in strange territory. In *The Comforters* Muriel Spark's heroine is haunted by peculiar voices, while Death makes telephone calls to geriatric patients in *Memento Mori.* But in another early novel by Spark a somewhat supernatural being actually appears in an industrial suburb of London. *The Ballad of Peckham Rye* provides a precise example of demonic didacticism in that moral instruction is offered by a trickster who may be the Devil himself. By making her devilish protagonist a Scot (named Dougal Douglas), Spark no doubt intends to delight any Calvinists in her audience. Although a playful spirit ripples over much of this work, an undercurrent of blood and violence frequently erupts, making the overall effect unsettling.

The basic situation recalls the demonic Honor Klein's crashing entry into the genteel world of Martin Lynch-Gibbon in Murdoch's *A Severed Head;* only now we are dealing mainly with the working classes rather than the more intellectual upper classes. But like Honor Klein, Dougal is an outsider who plunges into the community, stirs up a lot of mischief, and tears away illusions, forcing people to recognize the superficial nature of the flimsy structures they have tacked together to order their lives. But while Honor Klein influences Martin Lynch-Gibbon in an ultimately positive way, some of the characters in Spark's novel are shattered when they are made to view reality from a more illuminating perspective. In fact, some critics see Dougal simply as an evil force who wreaks destruction and chaos upon a formerly tranquil community.[1] More perceptive readers point out that Dougal really does no evil himself but merely acts as a catalyst for the evil churning under the respectable surfaces of society.[2] But only Karl Malkoff has recognized the morally instructive role that the demonic visitor plays: "What Dougal offers is freedom from the confines of artificial moralities; he preaches the respect for oneself that must precede respect for others."[3]

Honor Klein teaches a similar lesson to Martin Lynch-Gibbon, but Spark's book differs from Murdoch's in that the Scot's demonic traits are not just imagined in the mind of a fanciful first person narrator as in the case of Honor and Martin. In *The Ballad of Peckham Rye* the laconic third-person narrator reports that Dougal asks a number of different characters to feel the bumps where his horns were sawed off by a plastic surgeon. Dougal's hunched shoulders and claw-like right hand provide him with unnatural dexterity. And he describes dreams where he appears as the Devil. But Dougal also boasts about having powers of exorcism: "the ability to drive devils out of people." When reminded of his previous claim that he himself is the Devil, the didactic demon replies, "The two states are not incompatible."[4]

Playing with Dougal's diabolic nature throughout the novel, Spark offers just enough information so that we do not quite believe that Dougal is really the Devil nor do we quite believe that he isn't. As Malkoff points out, Dougal's identity remains ambiguous.[5] His aversion to sickness, for instance, can signify both a limited sense of compassion and a commitment to health and vitality. To add to the confusion, Dougal Douglas sometimes refers to himself as Douglas Dougal.

Another important difference between Murdoch's demonic professor and Spark's fey highlander is that while Honor Klein becomes intensely involved with two other characters, Dougal Douglas flits through the novel without establishing any serious relationships. On one hand, his detached manner seems to make him even more devilish, for perhaps only the devil would go to such lengths to cause trouble among people he doesn't really care about. On the other hand, it sometimes seems that Dougal wants to jolt the whole town into a new perception of moral values. It is he, for instance, who classifies the four types of morality observable in Peckham:

> Take the first category, Emotional. Here, for example, it is considered immoral for a man to live with a wife who no longer appeals to him. Take the second, Functional, in which the principal factor is class solidarity such as, in some periods and places, has also existed amongst the aristocracy, and of which the main manifestation these days is the trade union movement. Three, Puritanical, of which there are several modern variants, monetary advancement being the most prevalent gauge of the moral life in this category. Four, Traditional, which accounts for about one per cent of the Peckham population, and which in its simplest form is Christian. (*B*, 94)

Although here Dougal is trying to trick a prospective employer into believing he is an expert sociologist, he nevertheless shrewdly assesses that in the three most common moral attitudes in Peckham, human relationships are subordinated to other values, whether it be one's own emotional indulgences, class structure, or money.

One of the citizens of Peckham Rye who has subordinated the individual to other concerns, Mr. V. R. Druce presides as managing director of the local textile plant of Meadows, Meade, and Grindley. As Mr. Druce interviews Dougal for a job at the plant, he acts as a mouthpiece for company values. Sounding like the Director of Hatcheries in Huxley's *Brave New World,* Druce explains the company's training, recreation, and bonus schemes as well as its plans for a pension, marriage, and burial scheme. As a result of a visit from a "motion study" expert from Cambridge, the company's new motto becomes: "Conserve energy and time in feeding the line" (*B,* 18). But now Dougal Douglas is to be hired as an Arts man who will "bring vision into the lives of the workers" (*B,* 17). Just as the time-study man charted the efficiency level of the company, Dougal will now chart the workers' souls as he performs his "human research." As the managing director explains, "Our aim is to be one happy family" (*B,* 19).

While Druce continues to spit out platitudes, Dougal satirizes the shallow rhetoric with matching hackneyed phrases: "The World of Industry throbs with human life. It will be my job to take the pulse of the people and plumb the industrial depths of Peckham" (*B,* 18). Oblivious to the criticism, Druce seems intrigued by the curious man whose very appearance keeps altering. As Druce lectures on the organization of the company, Dougal mocks the very idea of structure by constantly modifying his own form. At one moment, "Dougal changed his shape and became a professor. He leaned one elbow over the back of his chair and reflected kindly upon Mr. Druce." At another moment, "Dougal leaned forward and became a television interviewer" (*B,* 17). Dougal's different poses hint that Druce himself wears a mask, but the managing director remains unaware of any implied criticism in the antics of his prospective employee. Indeed, as the relationship between the two men develops, Druce grows increasingly fond of the Scot as the director's very sexual orientation becomes uncertain. Even in this first interview, "Druce could not keep his eyes off Dougal" (*B,* 16). And later Dougal boasts, "I'm his first waking experience of an attractive man" (*B,* 112).

After he is hired, Dougal chats more intimately with the managing director, who by now begins to reveal the insecurity behind his official mask. While Druce pontificates about organizational skill and the "moral fibre" needed to "get on in business," his personal life lacks any real meaning, although here too he clings to artificial structures. His marriage is an empty form: he hasn't talked to his wife since the time five years ago when she mimicked him by quacking like a duck. Since then he only writes notes to her. It doesn't take Dougal long to figure out Druce's unethical motive for staying married. Now an inquisitor, he points an accusing finger at the managing director and states, "Mrs. Druce has got money" (B, 75). Putting his head on his desk, Druce ends the conversation by breaking into tears, while a co-worker observes, "This place is becoming chaos" (B, 76).

The statement could apply to both Honor Klein's and Dougal Douglas's attacks on the artificial forms that society erects to establish a semblance of order: chaotic destruction of superficial forms must precede the creation of true order. The citizens of Peckham Rye have adhered to artificial structures so rigidly that life in the community has become very mechanical. Workers at the textile plant, for instance, are usually associated with their menial assignments such as: "Dawn Waghorn, cone-winder . . . Odette Mill, uptwister . . . and Lucille Potter, gummer" (B, 14). People are thought of as machines and frequently act like machines. A businessman receives erotic thrills from riding up and down in a jerky elevator. The courting ritual of young people at a local dance hall resembles a series of mechanical actions:

> Most of the men looked as if they had not properly woken from deep sleep, but glided as if drugged, and with half closed lids, towards their chosen partner. This approach found favor with the girls. The actual invitation to dance was mostly delivered by gestures; a scarcely noticeable flick of the man's head towards the dance floor. Whereupon the girl, with an outstretched movement of surrender, would swim into the hands of the summoning partner. (B, 65)

The dancing itself becomes mechanical: when the music is interrupted, the couples "slowed down like an unwound toy roundabout" (B, 66).

In contrast to the mechanical forms that make the villagers so predictable, Dougal Douglas often jumps about like Pan in odd and unexpected ways: "Dougal sprang in the air and dipped with bent knees to illustrate his point, so that two or three people in the Old English garden turned to look at him" (B, 39). By his bizarre actions, Dougal criticizes society's slavish adherence to forms.

Similarly, although her book borrows elements from the ballad genre, Spark's own series of juxtaposed pictures, abrupt transitions, and multiple endings upset the reader's expectations about the form of a novel. Just as Dougal tries to jolt the villagers out of conventional behavior, so too Spark jerks the novel out of traditional molds.

Largely through Dougal, Spark also launches an attack on the mechanical forms of language used by the people of Peckham Rye. Dougal delights in revealing the shallow minds of the villagers by mimicking their speech patterns (B, 55). In addition he frequently uses non sequiturs to mock the insane rationalism of the industrial village (B, 83–84). Although Dougal undermines forms of language and behavior throughout the community, he makes direct impact upon a more limited number of individuals.

Besides Mr. Druce, Dougal's landlady Miss Belle Frierne proves to be another citizen of Peckham Rye whose complacency is severely disturbed by the town's curious young intruder. A symbol of respectability, Miss Frierne is known in the community as a proper lady with a "nice" rooming house on a pretty street with "neat" gardens (B, 21, 23). Having lived "up on the Rye" all her life in a house left by her father, Miss Frierne has become a neighborhood fixture. A woman at the meat market tells Dougal he'll be a lucky chap if Miss Frierne has a vacancy.

The name "Belle" ill fits a skinny old maid whose only contact with men results from her being their landlady. Yet she sees herself as a beauty pursued by male admirers, for her boarding house accommodates only gentlemen, whom she constantly protects by discouraging intrusive female visitors. Overnight guests are strictly forbidden, for in this proper establishment Miss Belle Frierne is the only lady allowed to approach the beds of her gentlemen boarders. And indeed on weekends, when the gentlemen are required to make their own beds, she often leaves little notes commenting on their efforts such as: "Today's bed was a landlady's delight. Full marks in your end-of-term report" (B, 43)!

Although Dougal becomes "lucky" enough to get a room in this establishment for "clean and go-ahead" young men and even acquires a good-bed report, he disturbs the aging belle when too early in the relationship he asks about her courting days. She turns away disdainfully, indicating "by various slight movements of her bony body that he had gone too far" (B, 44). About a month later, however, she reveals her one great sexual encounter, involving a Scottish soldier who grabbed her hand and stuck it up his kilt, causing Belle to scream so hard "that she had a quinsy for a week" (B, 44).

Although Belle has cultivated her role as a proper lady, her respectability remains as artificial as the imitation parquetry on her floors. Her drinking habits, for instance, qualify her decorum. Although she tries to be ladylike even as she indulges privately, sitting "primly up to the table with half a bottle of stout" (B, 43), when someone knocks on the front door, "Miss Frierne caused the bottle and glasses to disappear" (B, 136).

This correct old lady, "who had known all Peckham in her youth," symbolizes the town's hypocrisy, an aging drunk wearing a mask of gentility. At her bottle, she sighs over old memories and now leads a type of death-in-life existence, nicely suggested by her proper entry hall, "which was lined with wood like a coffin" (*B*, 141).

Belle's chance for life comes in the form of her long-lost brother who left home in 1919 but who suddenly pops up in town as an old derelict. While proud of her token symbols of generosity such as giving a dough-nut to a hungry boy, she nevertheless refuses to recognize her brother. "He was very shabby," she explains to Dougal, "and instinct made me stop" (*B*, 97). Although Dougal later tries to make a joke of the whole episode, he at first literally points his finger at Miss Frierne and chastises her for not acknowledging her brother. Nicely exemplifying the didactic demon, he even asks her to feel the bumps on his head as he lectures to her. Reacting to his candid and unsolicited moral instruction, Miss Frierne becomes flustered, cries, and warns that Dougal can find rooms elsewhere if he likes.

The scene is repeated when the brother appears again, but Miss Frierne is still too timid to let one of the memories of the good old days actually walk into her life.

When a policeman finally reports that he has found a body bearing a scrap of paper with her last name, Miss Frierne denies her brother even in death because she doesn't want to pay for his funeral. Here Dougal comments grimly, "Ever seen a corpse?" (*B*, 138). Imitating a dead man by lolling his head back and making his jaw rigid, he then proceeds to deliver his landlady into a state of hysteria.

When Miss Frierne herself soon approaches death by having a stroke, Dougal's moral lesson becomes even clearer. After the doctor asks him if "she has got any relatives," he utters a simple "No," just as she had recently done when asked if the dead man was her brother.

Another of Dougal's victims is Mr. Weedin, personnel manager at the textile plant of Meadows, Meade, and Grindley, who encounters his most difficult personnel problem in his new assistant, Dougal Douglas. Mr. Weedin cannot be called an "Arts man" like Dougal but is said to "know his job inside out" (*B*, 19). Mr. Weedin begins to fret, however, when six weeks after Dougal arrives, he notices that absenteeism has increased eight per cent. When Weedin calls attention to this problem, the manag-ing director, prompted by Dougal, suggests that things must get worse before they improve and that the personnel manager lacks vision. Weedin comes to believe that Dougal ultimately wants his job. Becoming more and more nervous, he finally confronts Dougal with his suspicion: "It isn't possible to get another good position in another firm at my age. . . . Druce is impossible to work for. It's impossible to leave this firm. Sometimes I think I'm going to have a breakdown" (*B*, 83). He does.

Spark refrains from providing much information about the personal life of the personnel manager probably because, like Mrs. Hogg in *The*

Comforters, he lacks one. Mr. Weedin instead seems to embody a paranoid sense of conformity. Constantly aware of other people being able to see him through the glass walls of his office, he suppresses any emotions or actions that could be considered unconventional.

He broods about Dougal so much, however, that he begins to see him not only as a threat to his job but also as a "diabolical agent, if not in fact the devil" (*B,* 92). But when he tells one of his co-workers of the bumps on Dougal's head, she merely reports to her boss, "Mr. Weedin will be wanting a holiday" (*B,* 93).

One of Dougal's aids in his "human research," Nelly Mahone re-mains—unlike so many of the other characters—essentially unchanged by the town's strange visitor. Nelly's stability probably results from the fact that she already falls outside the realms of convention and respect-ability. An old crone with long gray hair, she lives in a room whose filth shocks even a band of hoodlums. But as she tries to explain, "It's all clean dirt" (*B,* 106). Her description could apply to her moral nature as well. For even though Nelly is seen as a village idiot, she serves as a reminder of a spiritual order far removed from the petty concerns of many of the other characters. Dressed in rags, she lurks outside the pubs, screaming out passages from the Bible and praising "the Lord, almighty and eter-nal, wonderful in the dispensation of all his works" (*B,* 26).

Since she had "lapsed from her native religion on religious grounds" (*B,* 14), Nelly, considered a fanatic, is ignored by the rest of the town until she links up with the demonic visitor. Her unholy alliance ul-timately causes her to be brutalized by a group of young men, who suspect that Dougal is employed by an underworld gang and try to force information out of the queer old hag. Later when she meets Dougal on the street, she disguises a secret message about these thugs in biblical language. As well as assisting her devilish friend, Nelly Mahone, floating in and out of the plot with her mad religious utterances, serves as a ghostly chorus, implicitly criticizing the trivial activities of the other villagers. After she yells out messages from the spiritual world, she usually comments on the village by spitting on the street.

While Dougal causes little change in the life of Nelly Mahone, he alters profoundly the existence of the head typist at Meadows, Meade, and Grindley. Through several chats with Merle Coverdale, Dougal learns of her supposedly secret affair with Mr. Druce. Although Merle tells Dou-gal that the marriage between Druce and his wife must be considered "immoral" because "there's no feeling between them," almost in the same breath she admits that she herself has "fallen out of love with Mr. Druce" (*B,* 35) yet she cannot end their relationship. Dougal repeatedly urges Merle to assert her independence by asking questions like "Are you a free woman or a slave?" (*B,* 34, 100). But Merle explains that she continues with Druce because he helps pay for her flat and is responsible for her position at the plant. At thirty-eight, Merle feels she would be unable to secure another job of equal status.

Appropriately, as Merle describes her dead relationship with Mr. Druce, she and Dougal stroll through a cemetery. As they walk along, however, Dougal stops at one of the graves to perform more of his antics: "He posed like an angel-devil, with his hump shoulder and gleaming smile, and his fingers of each hand widespread against the sky" (*B*, 34). While Dougal acts like a demonic sprite, he also gets Merle to recognize the immoral nature of her relationship with Mr. Druce. When he tells her "you feel that you're living a lie," she admits, "I do . . . you've put my very thoughts into words" (*B*, 35). Besides being morally instructive, the devilish intruder also appeals to the primitive spirit locked inside the aging office worker: "Then she laughed her laugh from her chest, and Dougal pulled that blond front lock of her otherwise brown hair, while she gave him a hefty push such as she had not done to a man for twenty years" (*B*, 38).

Contrasting to the spontaniety between Merle and Dougal, the Saturday evenings shared by Merle and Mr. Druce move with piston-and-cylinder regularity. Like the gestures of the young people in the dance hall, here too actions and reactions are so well-rehearsed that they have become mechanical: "Presently Mr. Druce looked at his watch. At which Merle put down her knitting and switched on the television" (*B*, 58). The bedroom scene also conforms to a rigid pattern, as the monotonous symmetry of the prose suggests:

> Then they went into the bedroom and took off their clothes in a steady rhythm. Merle took off her cardigan and Mr. Druce took off his coat. Merle went to the wardrobe and brought out a green quilted silk dressing gown. Mr. Druce went to the wardrobe and found his blue dressing gown with white spots. Merle took off her blouse and Mr. Druce his waistcoat. (*B*, 60)

Even their sado-masochistic sexual activity follows a numerical formula: while in bed, Merle screamed "twice" because Mr. Druce had "once pinched her and once bit her." These expressions of endearment are bestowed routinely because Merle is "covered with marks" (*B*, 60). Echoing T. S. Eliot's account of another typist and clerk, Spark creates her own wasteland with dull verbs and repetitious clauses as she concludes one more Saturday night between the managing director and his mistress: "She went into the scullery and put on the kettle while he put on his trousers and went home to his wife" (*B*, 61).

The second account of another of these Saturday evenings sounds similar to the first, with the slight difference being that before Mr. Druce leaves, he picks up a corkscrew, stabs Merle in the neck nine times, and kills her. Spark makes the didactic point that, given the grotesquely static nature of the relationship, this minor alteration in their deadly routine hardly makes a difference. On one level, Dougal has triggered this deviation because Druce has become suspicious of the relationship between Merle and Dougal, who he finally believes has been spying on his business for the police. But one of the dominant motifs suggests that Druce has hated Merle all along. He is frequently shown pointing a sharp object in her direction: "He turned with the bottle-opener in his hand and looked at her" (B, 58); later "Mr. Druce took a bread-knife from the drawer and looked at her" (B, 59); and in the office, "Mr. Druce lifted his paper-knife; toyed with it in his hand, pointed it at Merle and put it down" (B, 93). Dougal's meddling may make the weapon ultimately find its home in Merle's neck, but since neither of the two characters had been vital enough to break out of the relationship as Dougal advised, the actual death seems healthier than the death-in-life pattern in which the two people had been trapped.

Unlike both Merle and Mr. Druce who at first found Dougal charming, Dixie Morse hates Dougal almost immediately. A typist at the textile plant, Dixie is engaged to "refrigerator engineer" Humphrey Place. Although she realizes Humphrey is influenced by his new neighbor, she remains unimpressed by Dougal's supernatural aura. Nor does Dougal ever single out Dixie for one of his long conversations probably because he senses that he could have little effect upon her implacable nature. Dixie Morse remains the most static character in the novel. From the first time we see her scrutinizing her bank book to the last days before her wedding when she reminds her fiancé that his company is offering "plenty of overtime," Dixie thinks mainly of saving her pennies. Her philosophy of life seems to be: "We need all the money we can get" (B, 140).

Even her sexuality is affected by her obsession as is suggested when she simultaneously jerks her hips and peruses her bank statement. During a tryst with Humphrey the conversation focuses on the pay raise that went to the personnel manager's daughter rather than to Dixie. Both her office work and her relationship with Humphrey suffer when she moonlights as an usherette at the local theater. During a rare night off to go to a pub with Humphrey and another couple, she orders ginger ale when Humphrey buys the round but switches to a more expensive mixed drink whenever the other fellow pays. Spark's relentless reminders of Dixie's penurious habits become almost tedious until one realizes that the author's purpose is to demonstrate the stultifying effect of such a stingy outlook.

Just as she keeps tight reins on her money so too is Dixie narrow-minded about other people, whom she likes to categorize. When she sees Dougal crying, for instance, she happily labels him a "pansy." She considers factory workers "lower class" and won't talk to them.

Dixie's limited perspective is reinforced by her mannerisms that suggest a trivial, self-absorbed mind: in one scene, "Dixie set one leg across the other, and watched the toe of her shoe, which she wriggled" (B, 11). A description of Dixie eating at a restaurant functions as an objective correlative for her meticulously frugal soul: she "touched the corners of her mouth with a paper napkin, and carefully picking up her knife and fork, continued eating, turning her head a little obliquely to receive each small mouthful" (B, 115). One senses that if Dixie marries Humphrey, she will eat him up in small mouthfulls too.

While Dixie remains egotistical and limited, Humphrey Place, although ordinary and practical, seems more sensitive toward others. In the scene where Dixie rudely files her nails while her mother reminisces about her romantic first marriage, Humphrey sits forward with a hand on each knee, feigning interest in order to compensate for Dixie's obvious indifference. He also defends Dougal's masculinity before Dixie and several others who question it. Thirdly, Humphrey becomes a spokesman for the traditional work ethic, insisting that "Absenteeism is downright immoral. Give a fair week's work for a fair week's pay" (B, 39). In addition, he frequently tries to act as peacemaker in barroom brawls although several times he finally becomes involved. Honest, upright, and sincere, Humphrey often serves as a scapegoat, the most vivid example being when his face is smashed by a broken beer glass intended for his friend. A barmaid tries to help Humphrey by "holding up to his face a large thick towel which was becoming redder and redder" (B, 124).

In spite of the pain he experiences in these barroom skirmishes, Humphrey is even more victimized in his relationship with Dixie Morse. He must listen to her constant preaching about the importance of saving money. He is allowed to go out with his fiancée only once a week so he too can save. For their mountain rendezvous he carries along two rugs, one for Dixie to sit upon and the other to put over her legs while he sprawls on the damp ground and listens to her complain about their finances. At a restaurant where the waitress spills the coffee into Dixie's saucer, he quickly exchanges cups of coffee, pours the spilled liquid into his cup, and downs it without saying a word. Through a number of such episodes it becomes clear that in their future marriage, Dixie will dominate and Humphrey will serve.

The situation is ripe for intervention. Strategically located just one floor above Humphrey in Miss Frierne's rooming house, Dougal frequently invites up the naive refrigerator repairman for talks lasting long into the night. The two men provide a study in contrast. While Humphrey talks seriously about trade unions, Dougal lolls on his bed and fiddles with a knob on the brass bedstead. After Humphrey earnestly expounds upon the worker's Conciliation Act of 1896 and the Industrial Court Act of 1919, Dougal starts to chatter about a mermaid who plays harp and writes poetry. Asking Humphrey if he would like to be married to such a mermaid, Dougal doesn't add "rather than Dixie," but Humphrey seems to understand his meaning. When Humphrey admits that such a union would be "fascinating," the demonic qualities of his new friend intensify: "Dougal gazed at Humphrey like a succubus whose mouth is its eyes" (B, 31). Humphrey's vulnerability makes him easy work for Dougal, whose influence is seen almost immediately. After Dougal suggests that Dixie could be considered "lower middle class" rather than just "middle class," Humphrey at first looks insulted, "but then he looked pleased. His eyes went narrow, his head lolled on the back of the chair, copying one of Dougal's habitual poses" (B, 33). While the Dionysian conductor of human research pours wine down Humphrey's throat and even entertains him with a sprightly dance or two, Humphrey begins to slip off his rigid Apollonian demeanor: "Humphrey laughed deeply with his head thrown back . . . so Dougal could see the whole inside of his mouth" (B, 55). As a result of his talks with Dougal, Humphrey becomes increasingly critical of Dixie, accusing her of losing her sexuality because of her preoccupation with money. When she harps that they will not be able to afford a new spin-dryer, Humphrey boldly proclaims, "Oh to hell with your spin-dryer" (B, 62).

As Dougal continues to stir up the placid waters of Humphrey's soul, he even asks the innocent refrigerator repairman to feel the two bumps on his head. But refusing to recognize the demonic nature of his new friend, Humphrey suggests that the bumps are simply "a couple of cysts" (B, 86) rather than sawed-off horns.

Dougal performs his most devilish mischief, however, on the night that he mocks a traditional wedding ceremony by pretending to be a groom who, when asked the crucial question, says, "No." Although Humphrey laughs off Dougal's derisive performance, the seed is planted. Shortly thereafter during his own wedding ceremony, when the minister asks if he will take Dixie as his wife, this polite young man distinctly states: "No, to be quite frank, I won't" (B, 158). He then leaves town, again imitating his friend Dougal, who has become very unpopular among the citizens of Peckham Rye.

Although the last chapter remains inconclusive, many townspeople attest that Humphrey returned and finally married Dixie with a crowd of uninvited guests waiting around the church to see if he would say no again. Even though his influence may have been temporary, Dougal

Douglas did make a conventional young man perform an act of daring individuality that could have liberated him from a long oppressive relationship. Probably as a result of Dougal's influence this usually unimaginative young man at least glimpses at a more idealistic world as he experiences his most visionary moment. The book's last words reflect Humphrey's point of view: "It was a sunny day for November, and, as he drove swiftly past the Rye, he saw the children playing there and the women coming home from work with their shopping bags, the Rye for an instant looking like a cloud of green and gold, the people seeming to ride upon it, as you might say there was another world than this" (*B*, 160). The other world represents a higher spiritual plane that strangely enough may have been revealed to Humphrey by the Devil himself.

A VISIT FROM THE GRAVE
The Public Image

A productive year for Muriel Spark, 1960 saw the publication of both *The Ballad of Peckham Rye* and *The Bachelors*. Like the former novel, *The Bachelors* contains supernatural elements such as a medium who foams at the mouth and twitches when under the influence of a "control" from the other world. Another character also foams ostensibly because he suffers from epilepsy. Although the two figures parallel each other in several ways, the latter, significantly named Ronald Bridges, makes important moral connections between the material and spiritual worlds. Even though his malady overwhelms him from time to time so that a friend thinks he is "possessed by the devil,"[1] Bridges gains from his terrifying convulsions a keen sense of ethics which makes him a severe judge of his companions: "But it is all demonology, he thought, and he brought them all to witness, in his old style, one by one, before the courts of his mind."[2] Once again Spark uses a personality with a "diabolical side to his nature"[3] as a mouthpiece for her moral statements. But this work abandons the industrial suburb of Peckham Rye for the apartments and flats of Chelsea, Hampstead, and Kensington, wherein reside a large number of odd people, many of whom are unmarried. The author's extensive collection of characters—including poor young men, wealthy old ladies, pregnant waitresses, art critics, clairvoyants, phony priests, and pornographers—makes her work confusing even though she tries to connect her eccentrics through a court case involving the quivering medium.

Muriel Spark's 1968 novel also explores communication between the natural and supernatural world but involves fewer characters and remains more lucid in its design. *The Public Image* represents a ghost story for the machine age in that one of the central characters does not really exist but is an illusion conjured in the magical foundry of modern cinematography. Called "The English Tiger-Lady," a provocative screen personality is created from a mousy British actress named Annabel Christopher, whose "eyes were not large, but on the screen . . . came out so, by some mystery."[4]

Set in Rome, the film capital of Europe, the novel examines the movie making industry, where reality becomes lost in a forest of illusion. Like Iris Murdoch's novels, Spark's *The Public Image* points to the danger involved when a concept about a person becomes more important than the person herself. In this novel, however, the author also shows that technology can magnify and reproduce the concept so that an entire populace can be "enchanted" by an artificial image imposed upon a real person.

Like Mischa Fox in *The Flight from the Enchanter,* Annabel Christopher uses the myth that has enveloped her to gain money and recognition, but while Murdoch demonstrates how Mischa exploits others, Spark emphasizes how Annabel herself is victimized by her public image. This "little tale of Twentieth Century demonology," as one critic has called the novel,[5] turns into a battle for survival between Annabel Christopher and the celluloid ghost who more and more overshadows the real woman. Believing that personality amounts to the effect one has upon others, Annabel's movie producer Luigi Leopardi tells her, "It's what I began to make of you that you've partly become" (*PI,* 37). Although Annabel could be called "a little slip of a thing," her face has changed "as if by the action of many famous cameras into a mould of her public figuration" (*PI,* 39). While her smile had formerly been quick and small, now it is "slow and somewhat formal." In her new role she looks vivacious only when the time [comes] in front of the cameras, to play the tiger" (*PI,* 39).

Annabel's image as "The English Tiger-Lady" evolves from a series of second-rate films in which Luigi Leopardi somehow transformed this nondescript player of minor parts into a charismatic film star, whose polite demeanor supposedly forms only a facade for the smoldering sensuality within.

Although her more intellectual husband Frederick, a failed actor and occasional scriptwriter, believes Annabel to be shallow through and through, he at first cooperates in the development of his wife's public image. In fact, Leopardi's press agent, Francesca, takes on both Annabel and Frederick Christopher as her special assignment. Through a series of carefully staged photographs in the Italian film magazines Francesca creates the ideal married couple who form the perfect blend of daytime decorum and nocturnal passion. In one magazine Francesca has the English couple photographed

> with a low table set with a lace-edged tray of afternoon tea, and the sun streaming in the window. Frederick held his cup and seemed to be stirring it gently and gravely while Annabel, sweet but unsmiling touched the silver teapot with a gracious hand. (*PI,* 28–29)

Yet in another magazine Francesca makes her assistant

take a picture of Annabel lounging on the bed in her nightdress, one shoulder-band slipping down her arm and her hair falling over part of her face. Francesca disarranged the bed. She sat Frederick on the edge of the bed, in a Liberty dressing-gown, smoking, with a smile as of recent reminiscence. (*PI*, 28)

A crucial part of this public image is that the tiger-sex be confined to the marital bed. With words that remind us of Calvin Blick's camera work in *The Flight from the Enchanter*, Robert Ostermann has commented on this photogenic couple: "so deeply is each partner implicated in this 'public image' of Annabel as Tiger that together they are trapped, held together like a photograph of perfection permanently sealed in plastic, to be forever admired but untouched."[6] Although their motives are different, both Francesca and Calvin Blick try to freeze contingent reality into a fixed form. Both try to confine life into the neat parameters of one dominant image.

As in Murdoch's novel, the image here too involves a deception. In spite of a recent attempt to mend their marriage with a new baby, Frederick and Annabel now seldom sleep together; each has had affairs; and they remain together only out of convenience. But while Annabel becomes obsessed with preserving her public image, Frederick grows increasingly rebellious. Deeply disturbed that his limited wife should achieve such fame, Annabel's husband feels that his own great talent has never been discovered.

In the early part of the novel, the omniscient narrator satirizes Frederick's great talent, "so far as talent, continually unapplied, can be said to exist" (*PI*, 8). Unable to develop his acting career, he also seems unable to control his lust: "Frederick hardly knew what was going on. He was still fascinated by Francesca, and then he was fascinated by her plump sister who had an indeterminate clerical job in a back office of the film studios, and then he was attracted to her fair, lean brother for whom Francesca was trying hard to get a part in a film" (*PI*, 27). In contrast to the formlessness in Frederick's own life, the structure of his new public image grows. Annabel and Frederick are photographed on their walks around Rome as they "leant on monuments, dallied at fountains," or appeared "together as the marvellous couple with the secret of happy marriage, on the Spanish Steps" (*PI*, 36). In spite of the serene public image, "Frederick's misery began to show in his face" (*PI*, 32).

As he is absorbed into the role of the Tiger-Lady's husband, he feels as if the movie company is writing a script for his life. In order to resist this process he finally decides to throw out the company's script and write his own.

The plot of Frederick's new script is based upon the destruction of the

Tiger-Lady. Frederick chooses a diabolic method to attack his wife's public image by creating yet another phantom to combat, as Melvin Maddocks has said, "the living ghost his wife is becoming."[7] Frederick Christopher is transformed into a didactic demon when he kills himself to teach his wife a lesson. Much more powerful as a phantom than as the flesh-and-blood husband who sulked as he lived off his wife's money, Frederick's ghost sets a series of traps from which even the Tiger-Lady may not be able to extricate herself. He has arranged that at the exact time he is killing himself an orgy take place at his wife's new apartment, and he has even invited members of the press. Five suicide notes charging that his wife's licentious living drove him to despair are strategically placed so that discovery will be inevitable. One of them is addressed to his "Dearest Momma," who actually died several years before, but Frederick knows that passionate letters from sons to mothers (living or dead) are given special coverage in the journals of Italy, the "Motherland of Sensation" (PI, 26). Thus Frederick's ghost is dedicated to the task of spilling blood on his wife's public image, and the actress must employ all the resources of her profession in order to keep her image intact. A large part of the rest of the novel describes the fierce and ingenious struggle the Tiger-Lady wages to avoid the deadly snares her demonic husband has set for her. But ultimately Frederick's wife learns that the Tiger-Lady must indeed die in order for Annabel Christopher to live.

Even though the book moves swiftly, not unlike a movie with its series of dramatic scenarios, the author makes her short novel intriguing by allowing several different interpretations. In this work about images and movies Spark seems to invite the reader as well as Frederick to choose among several different versions of the script. This ambiguity, of course, also contributes to the novel's surrealistic shading.

We are never quite sure, for instance, why Annabel's husband acts as he does. Although Frederick turns out to be a didactic demon, he may not have intended to be one. Spark makes his motivation somewhat mysterious. Frederick may have meant to be purely demonic: an avenging fury returning from the grave to destroy his wife. The suicide notes and the vulgar party he organizes suggest that he acts out of jealousy and hatred. To haunt his wife more, he may even have sent along an attendant spirit in the form of the doctor's little daughter Gelda, who at a public gathering makes cynical comments about the Tiger-Lady. When Annabel weeps for Frederick, for instance, Gelda chirps, "The actresses can make themselves cry, they have to learn how to do it" (PI, 75). Annabel then "turned with a horrified gasp on her cynical enemy; she had discerned an echo of Frederick's voice" (PI, 75). Reminders of her husband lurk everywhere. After his death Frederick's threatening presence becomes so pervasive that Annabel begins to think of him as still alive.

At one point she reflects "that Frederick would have to be warned not to speak of the party" (*PI*, 83). Although she suddenly remembers that Frederick has died, she often continues to speak of her husband in the present tense: she demands to see the suicide letters because she "want[s] to know what he's trying to do" (*PI*, 90). Upon reading the letters to his mother, she similarly declares, "He must be mad" (*PI*, 93). Thus the Tiger-Lady prepares for battle with a very vital ghost: "She [sits] up to hear the rest, fully strained towards the professional nature of the enemy, desiring only to know the full extent and scope of his potential force" (*PI*, 96). When she sees that his handwriting on the suicide notes seems perfectly normal and not in the least bit shaky, she concludes, "He's dangerous" (*PI*, 96). The nightmarish problems that the demonic husband creates for his wife could indeed suggest that Frederick has been inspired by hatred and envy.

On the other hand, one might wonder if this man could have been so jealous of his wife that he would go to such lengths simply out of cynical revenge. Moved by a strange love rather than hate, could he have wanted to save Annabel from her own public image? Can his deeds, like those of Honor Klein, be seen as acts of positive destruction? Critics have called attention to the fact that Frederick's last name of Christopher means Christ-bearer. And his suicide assumes symbolic overtones when he jumps to his death at the site of the martydom of Saint Paul. His wife can never understand why he chooses a location so colored by religious history. Like the early Christians, does he too sacrifice himself in a martyr's death? This more positive interpretation of Frederick's deed is certainly kept in the background, but even Annabel admits that there exists a "vast unknown" about Frederick that "she had never explored" (*PI*, 66).

Although Spark employs an omniscient narrator, Annabel becomes the center of consciousness; therefore, much of our knowledge of Frederick is shaped by her perspective. In fact, Frederick never appears "on stage" during the four-day time span of the novel's main action (just as Peter Crean-Smith never made a "live appearance" in the central plot of *The Unicorn*). Frederick's absence from the "present tense" of the novel suggests that the whole relationship between husband and wife depends upon illusion. We learn about Frederick largely through flashbacks as well as through Annabel's troubled musings. And most of Annabel's worries about Frederick while he still lives result from his being essential to her public image.

Just as one can never be sure whether Frederick intends moral instruction in his demonism, his character ultimately remaining as mysterious as the ghost he becomes, so too Annabel herself is presented in ambivalent terms. Certainly she as well as Frederick is often described with sarcasm: she sometimes seems as stupid as Frederick had accused her of being. For instance, when her old friends insist that she has a talent for solving problems, "she was not sure that they were not right because she was not sure what a problem was" (*PI*, 40). Although hardly guilty of the licentious behavior depicted in the suicide notes and preferring her sexual activity "under the covers . . . with her nightgown on" (*PI*, 116), Annabel has on occasion broken her marriage vows. Here too the narrator delights in sardonic description. Having received an amorous invitation from one of Frederick's friends, Annabel "responded idly with two afternoons in bed with him, after which they got dressed and made the bed" (*PI*, 6).

Robert Kiely has argued that Spark's protagonist remains uninteresting because her private life is as shallow and false as her public life.[8] But Spark tries to show that if one is obsessed with cultivating an image, the self behind the mask does not have the time or energy to develop into a real person. In the Tiger-lady's new hectic life, "Time became a hunted animal" (*PI*, 15). In earlier days Annabel had enjoyed the simple pleasure of writing a letter to her grandfather, walking to the post office, buying one stamp, and dropping the letter into the box. Now a secretary answers the Tiger-Lady's voluminous mail more or less as she pleases. Thus the professional mask of the actress begins to smother the real self. But Kiely does not notice Annabel's potential for freedom and growth.

The protagonist undergoes a constant struggle between a real woman who vaguely yearns for a simpler, more natural life and an artificial woman whose existence depends upon an intricate network of deception and stifled impulses. Annabel's character gains complexity as the author's treatment of her alternates between sympathy and scorn.

Spark creates a certain amount of empathy for Annabel by surrounding her with less appealing characters, such as Billy O'Brien, a parasite who has been hanging onto the couple for about eleven years. A friend of Frederick, Billy is tolerated by Annabel because he provides her with information about her husband. She even frequently depends on Billy to help her learn the whereabouts of her dissolute mate.

While Billy indirectly assists in preserving her image as the happily married Tiger-Lady, he also disturbs her quiet private existence as Annabel Christopher. In an early scene, he enters her new apartment without knocking and demands food and money. Before Billy's appearance Annabel had been contemplating the sunlight falling on her baby Carl in a room "at the back of the building, removed from the more roisterous traffic of Rome" (*PI*, 4). Here Spark provides a few glimpses of a real woman enjoying simple pleasures: "She could have prolonged for ever the lonely happiness of the early afternoon before Billy had arrived, with the baby sleeping on the floor, and nothing to do but wait for the furniture, feed and change the baby, bathe the baby" (*PI*, 47). This particular apartment especially suggests the possibility of an independent private life for Annabel because for the first time she has arranged the purchase of an apartment all by herself and has even managed to get a fairly reasonable price.

But her public image dictates that she cannot keep intruders out, and Billy O'Brien proves to be only the first among many obnoxious visitors. Through a series of images Spark depicts Billy as a greasy character. One of Billy's first temporary jobs involves slicing bacon; in this early scene in Annabel's new apartment he smears bacon fat on her movie script as he gorges himself at her table (*PI*, 46); later he gets similar stains on an important letter: "somehow or other he got a butter mark on it" (*PI*, 133). The imagery foreshadows Billy's ultimate attempt to soil the Tiger-Lady's public image by blackmailing her with copies of the suicide letters, which he discovers before the police.

Spark also draws sympathy for Annabel in the surrealisic orgy scene where a troupe of revelers right out of Fellini's *La Dolce Vita* invade her quiet apartment. Equipped with liquor and a noisy record player, the group multiplies in a dream-like way as Annabel hears "voices, more voices at the door" (*PI*, 51). Faces resemble the distorted images in a fun house mirror as one man "fresh from a drug feast" smiles uncontrollably (*PI*, 52). In the midst of screaming dancers, a gray-haired woman slinks about wearing a black dress with a large hole stretching obscenely from her waist to her thighs: "Annabel could never be quite sure, afterwards, if this woman, incongruously snaking her body with the young, had been real or imagined" (*PI*, 53). Just as Billy soiled her new apartment, this crowd also leaves its mark: "The mess was everywhere. The new wallpaper was no longer new. . . . Someone had been abundantly sick in one of the sinks" (*PI*, 59). And just as her real self yearned to revolt against Billy, here too Annabel wants to "villify everyone" and send them all packing. But since the visitors say they were sent by her husband for a surprise house warming party, the actress must be civil in order to preserve her image as a happy wife: "These people must not be allowed to know that she had no idea where Frederick had been, or that she was waiting for his return with any anxiety" (*PI*, 52). So the Tiger-Lady again plays hostess to vulgar intruders while Annabel carries her baby to a remote part of the apartment and then secretly empties four bottles of vodka down the toilet to hasten the end of this lurid nightmare.

While the narrator shows concern for the victimized Annabel and her baby during the orgy scene, his attitude becomes more critical during the farcical press conference that the Tiger-Lady holds in her apartment at 2:00 A.M. on the same night that her husband has killed himself. She decides to meet the reporters at this unearthly hour in hopes of wiping away the smudge her husband's suicide has made upon her public image before the story reaches the newsstands the next morning. She hopes to set the proper tone right away with a lavish display of grief and proclamations that her husband's death must have been an accident, for she would "never believe it was suicide," a phrase that her producer thinks will be a great line for one of her future movies. To form a buffer between herself and the press, Annabel calls upon her neighbors, who with an instinct for drama arrange a large semicircle of chairs, reserving for Annabel and her baby a plush red velvet seat resembling a throne. "Arranged as it was, with Annabel and infant in its midst" the scene resembles "some vast portrayal of a family and household by Holbein" (*PI*, 82). Flanked by sympathetic admirers, the Tiger-Lady plans to ward off embarrassing questions about an orgy in her apartment earlier that evening. Spark uses this scene to satirize the ghoulish press who feed on people's misfortunes, the Tiger-Lady and her obsessive concern for her public image at such a time, and even the neighbors themselves, who are more aware of the television camera than the tragedy: the men "had taken advantage of the furniture-fetching to brush their hair and shoes and to put on a respectable necktie" (*PI*, 76). When the reporters finally surge into the room: "Annabel blinked away her eyes' moisture, swallowed visibly, looked down at the baby and sighed" (*PI*, 78).

Although the press conference can be considered the Tiger-Lady's masterpiece of deception, she is constantly forced to engage in petty acts of concealment and subterfuge. She must often whisper to Billy or to one of Frederick's ex-mistresses so that the nurse in the next room, the babysitter with little Carl, or the neighbors behind the closed doors in her hallway will not overhear the elaborate plans that must be followed to preserve her public image. She stuffs the suicide letters under the bedcovers as a servant enters the room; she speaks a foreign language so that another employee will not understand. Goaded by her demonic husband's treachery, she experiences a vision of evil that necessitates paranoid strategies: she imagines "the poisoner behind the black window-square, a man flattened against a wall with the daggers ready . . . calumny, calumny, a messenger here and there, many messengers, bearing whispers and hints. . . . Fixed inventions of deeds not done, accusations, the determined blackening of character" (*PI*, 68–69).

Meanwhile the public sees only sorrow as "the cameras whine" (*PI*, 120) and the Tiger-Lady's producer plans to direct the "inquest like a movie" (*PI*, 135). Caught in this self-imposed network of petty intrigue and duplicity, the woman inside occasionally looks outward. One night after quarreling with Billy and her producer, "Annabel gazed out through the open window at the stars" (*PI*, 136). After a stormy session in the courtroom she rests her eyes upon "the young green trees beyond" (*PI*, 141). After being badgered by a group of reporters, she stares out a hotel window at a man below who seems to think that she could come down like "an ordinary free woman" (*PI*, 86). In another episode Annabel stands by her window watching a "cafe with the free young people sitting outside" (*PI*, 130). The pattern of entrapment here recalls Hannah Crean-Smith, who was also locked up in an intricate system of images; in one section Annabel is even described as being stifled by "the whole mythology which had vapoured so thickly about her" (*PI*, 32). Earlier Frederick had said, "If we don't draw the line now, they've got us trapped" (*PI*, 32). Although Frederick's method of "drawing the line" is quite bizarre, he ultimately forces Annabel to respect the differences between illusion and reality.

Her baby Carl also helps her to appreciate this distinction. Except for her desperate press conference, Annabel insists that the baby be kept out of the artificial arena of the Tiger-Lady. Annabel had warned that Francesca would be fired if she tried to bring the baby "into this parade" (*PI*, 36). In her love for her child, Annabel at least temporarily escapes her obsessive concern for her public self:

> The baby, Carl, was the only reality of her life. His existence gave her a sense of being permanently secured to the world which she had not experienced since her own childhood had passed. She was so enamoured of the baby that she did not want to fuss over it with gurgles and baby-babble, as did the nurse and the secretaries who came from the studio. She felt a curious fear of display where the baby was concerned, as if this deep and complete satisfaction might be disfigured or melted away by some public image (*PI*, 38).

One of the brightest moments of the novel occurs when, all alone, Annabel watches her baby play with a small ribbon before falling off to sleep. The innocent, spontaneous child symbolizes the contingency that the Tiger-Lady has not yet molded into the rigid form of her public personality. But when Annabel is forced to whisper once too often, when she is locked up with one greasy guest too many, and when she is pushed to her limits with Billy's treacherous attempt to blackmail her, she finally breaks that form herself and decides "I want to be free like my baby" (*PI*, 142).

At the inquest she therefore reveals Frederick's suicide letters, walks out of the amazed courtroom, removes her dark glasses, and unnoticed by any mob, leaves with her baby on an airplane bound for Athens. Frederick's deadly lesson has finally made its full impact: his wife realizes that only by destroying her public image can she herself be free. Although Annabel's child pointed to the doorway, it was her demonic husband who taught her that the structure of illusion enclosing her had become a horror house.

6

HELL-HOUSE
Not to Disturb

From the rigid structure of illusion surrounding Annabel Christopher in *The Public Image,* we move to a much more literal edifice that acts as the principal setting for a novel offering a searing vision of hell. The inhabitants of the baronial chateau in Muriel Spark's 1971 novel, *Not to Disturb,* could very well be creatures from the underworld. Although this dark book reflects mainly the narrow perspective of the bloodthirsty servants, no one demonic character serves as a didactic agent providing moral instruction. Like T. S. Eliot, Spark instead creates clear, sharp images of a hellish environment where the ethical statement is expressed more by what is absent than by what is present. In fact, echoes of *The Waste Land* can be heard throughout Spark's novel. The intellectual butler says, "How like . . . the death wish is to the life urge! How urgently does an overwhelming obsession with life lead to suicide! Really, it's best to be half-awake and half-aware. That is the happiest stage."[1] The latter two sentences, so applicable to a number of Spark's more mindlessly evil servants, also describe the death-in-life existence which Eliot saw as the human condition in modern times. The warm "Half-awake . . . half-aware" little life of those "dried tubers" causes Eliot's modern woman to ask her enervated husband, "Are you alive, or not? Is there nothing in your head?"[2] Spark's shallow servants recall the spiritually dead inhabitants of *The Waste Land.* Indeed, Spark may very well have been thinking of Eliot's characters when she has the butler look out the window at some people waiting in a car and say, "Good night, ladies. Good night sweet, sweet ladies" (*ND,* 13). His words, so similar to the last lines of the pub scene in "A Game of Chess," take on additional ironies when we realize that one of Spark's ladies is actually a transvestite. While Eliot's pub dwellers frivolously discuss abortion, false teeth, and "hot gammon," Spark's servants chatter happily about murder, death, and casseroles.

In both Eliot and Spark a bleak atmosphere and characters who in their insensitivity become more spectral than human underline the qualities of compassion and integrity by their conspicuous absence. Refuting the writer who found "no serious concern"[3] in Spark's book, a perceptive critic has said: "The blooming thing scares the reader; he may not be so terribly preposterous as anybody made up by Muriel Spark but he belongs to a race that can reach these depths and that thought is as profoundly affecting as kinship with Lear or Hamlet."[4] Or as a line from one of Spark's earlier novels puts it: "A vision of evil may be as effective to conversion as a vision of good."[5]

In some ways *Not to Disturb* also bears resemblance to Iris Murdoch's *The Unicorn.* The Gothic setting offers one of the major points of comparison. Much of the action in Murdoch's novel takes place in Gaze Castle, a huge old house located on a remote seascape frequently clouded over by mist and fog. A severe storm also forms an important part of both the literal and mythical landscape. In Spark's novel almost all the action occurs in the Klopstock chateau located on the edge of Lake Leman, which sends layers of fog rolling over the ancestral estate, while thunder can be heard "batting among the mountain-tops like African drums" (*ND*, 81).

While Murdoch makes special use of the storm as a counterpart to the calamitous events that develop during the long night's vigil at the end of *The Unicorn,* Spark compresses the action of the entire novel into one stormy nightwatch inside the sprawling chateau, which is disturbed by thunder, lightning, and a terrific wind that keeps banging the shutters. Since the entire novel is set in one time and place, Spark's book suggests a microcosm even more strongly than Murdoch's.

The sense of imprisonment, reinforced in *The Unicorn* by the imagery of locked bedrooms and bookcases, also prevails in *Not to Disturb.* While Hannah Crean-Smith was immured in Gaze Castle, here too various doors and gates lock people out or in. The entire estate is surrounded by a great fence whose gate is locked or unlocked by a docile porter who takes all his directions from the butler. Just as Rochester's mad wife in *Jane Eyre* was kept in a room at the top of the house, here also a demented relative called "him in the attic" must be incarcerated. Frequently strange sounds emanate from the idiot's enclosure: "At that moment a long wail comes from the top of the house, winding its way down the well of the stairs, followed then by another, winding through all the bannisters and seeping into the servants' hall" (*ND*, 66). A young couple who approach the chateau in an attempt to rescue their friend also ultimately find themselves confined within the gates of the estate on a stormy night. Most important, the book's title refers to the Baron and Baroness who along with their secretary have locked themselves within the library, demanding very emphatically that they are "not to be disturbed" (*ND*, 27).

The imprisonment imagery in *The Unicorn* suggests that characters were locked within obsessive relationships; similarly in Spark's novel all the locked doors emphasize the rigid patterns controlling the characters behind those doors. The central pattern involves the bloody drama that will be performed behind the bolted doors of the library when the Baron Klopstock confronts the Baroness with Victor Passerat, who has served as secretary and lover to both of his employers. Recalling the networks within the complex alliances of Murdoch's characters, Spark's novel also revolves around a fairly complicated relationship. As one of the more clever servants says, "To put it squarely . . . the eternal triangle has come full circle" (*ND* 29). But while some of the retainers in *The Unicorn* tried to prevent the bloody catastrophe that would ensue when Peter Crean-Smith returned to Gaze Castle, here the servants add catalysts to hurry along the violent reaction that will result from the explosive mixture of these three personalities. And while Murdoch's servants were often deeply and mysteriously attached to various members of the higher class, in *Not to Disturb* the servants have in no way committed themselves emotionally to their lords and ladies even though they have physically coupled with them in a variety of methods. Although hellish in many ways, Spark's menials, unlike the passionate slaves in *The Unicorn*, suggest little demons who devilishly dance about the dying bodies of their masters. But far more like vampires than any of the characters in *The Unicorn*, Spark's servants exploit the tragic situation by arranging to sell the magazine and movie rights before the sensational story even unfolds. Rather than cringe in anguish, the servants in Spark's book ghoulishly spend the night posing for photographs, reciting their memoirs into tape recorders, and rehearsing the stories they will tell the police in the morning. Thus the vision of hell in this novel terrifies the reader more than even the darkest shadows of *The Unicorn*. But perhaps Spark herself must be called the real demon because in an ironic yet macabre manner she tells this grim tale of violence and death as if she is relating an amusing anecdote at a cocktail party. The author seems to be enjoying herself immensely as she describes the games the servants play while their masters are killing themselves. The enormous incongruity between tone and event, however, may ultimately be part of Spark's didactic plan. In playing so devilishly with her sorry story she perhaps shocks us even more than she would if she had conveyed the gruesome plot in a direct rather than oblique fashion. Although the denizens of the strange Chateau Klopstock suggest caricatures instead of real people, Spark's bizarre vision becomes disturbingly instructive. In fact, Patricia Meyer Spacks explains the process of demonic didacticism when she writes about this book: "The reader's 'learning' consists in the revelation that the world he inhabits and imagines and peruses in his newspapers is as grotesque as that of the Gothic novel."[6]

The director of the diabolical drama to be performed in the Klopstock chateau on this stormy evening is Lister, the butler. Phrases such as "Leave it to Lister" or "Listen to Lister" form one of the dominant rhythms of the novel as periodically the "other servants fall silent as Lister enters the room" (*ND*, 56, 26, 3). This witty, intellectual servant who quotes Andrew Marvell, John Webster, Edward Fitzgerald, and James Shirley as easily as he reviews a grocery list not only sets the stage for the bloody performance that will take place behind the locked doors of the library but also sees to it that all distractions are kept off stage. Lister's obsessive concern with the meticulous order of the violent events that he has helped organize makes him truly demonic. His rigid attention to form and appearance can be seen throughout the novel. In the cloakroom Lister "arranges the neat unused hand-towels with the crested 'K' even more neatly" while "him in the attic" howls (*ND*, 11). At the large kitchen cupboard that hides his wall safe, Lister "carefully, one by one, removes the neat jars of preserved fruit that are stacked there" (*ND*, 12). Even Spark's sentence structure with its parallel series of verb phrases emphasizes the rational, step-by-step method in which Lister imposes apparent order upon chaos. After he has received some black-mail money, Lister

> then opens wide the safe which is neatly stacked with various enve-lopes and boxes, some of metal, some of leather. He places the new package among the rest, closes the safe, replaces the wooden shelf, and assisted by [two other servants], puts the preserve-bottles back in their places. He descends from his chair, hands the chair to [an assistant], closes the cupboard door, and goes to the window. (*ND*, 13)

The butler remains so certain that his bloody drama will be performed as planned that he often uses the past tense when talking about his employer. After all, for Lister the detail that the Baron still lives becomes a mere matter of "vulgar chronology" (*ND*, 49). Thus Lister's memoirs up to the funeral are "as a matter fact more or less complete" (*ND*, 8). The "more or less" refers to any contingent elements that might interfere with Lister's design. As he admits, "there was sure to be something unexpected" (*ND*, 8). But Lister proves to be a master at shaping contingency, at wrapping up all the ragged ends to fit into his demonic vision of reality. As the parlor maid explains in her own special language, "Lister can adjust whatever it is. Lister never disparates; he symmetrizes" (*ND*, 73).

One disparate element that almost upsets Lister's design involves the pertinent news that the rightful heir to the Klopstock estate happens to be the barking idiot in the attic. Here Lister's masterwork of modification emerges as a scheme to marry off the lunatic to the pregnant parlor maid, Heloise, who will still be under Lister's control even when she presides as the new baroness. But before this farce takes place, the heirs who still remain technically alive must first be admitted to the place of execution.

When the doorbell of the Klopstock mansion rings for the first time that evening, Lister receives Victor Passerat, a fair "long-locked young man . . . wearing a remarkable white fur coat which makes his pink skin somewhat radiant" (*ND,* 9). This exquisitely dressed young man in his blue satin suit and white cravat "fixed with an amethyst pin" has enchanted both the Baroness and the Baron and therefore feels superior to Lister as he hands him his coat "which speaks volumes" (*ND,* 86) and asks for the Baroness "in the quiet voice of one who does not wish to spend much of it" (*ND,* 9). But the fact that he serves as a pawn in Lister's elaborate chess game is suggested when Lister guides him across the black and white "chequered paving" of the hall that leads to the fateful library. We also learn of the active part the butler has played in manipulating and exploiting the tangled relationships of his employers when Passerat informs him that he will find the envelope with blackmail money "In the left-hand outer pocket, this time, Lister" (*ND,* 10). Once Passerat is admitted to the library, Lister tells the other servants that "Number one . . . walked to his death most gingerly" (*ND,* 11).

We thus do not really see much of the attractive secretary, his characterization being somewhat flat—a pretty image rather than a complex personality. In subsequent conversations among the other servants we learn that he was promiscuous but not especially well-liked. Heloise says about Victor, "I never went with him . . . I had the chance though" while the handyman responds, "Didn't we all?" (*ND,* 11).

If this glamorous servant insinuated himself until he became the favorite of both Baronness and Baron, his name Victor ultimately becomes ironic: once he is locked in the library, we do not see him again until the next morning when he lies "curled against a bookcase which is well splashed with his blood" (*ND,* 111–12).

Before long Lister escorts two more people to the library. Although the Baron and Baroness may seem to be victims of their conniving servants, they are hardly exempt from the vices and follies of their employees, whom they have exploited in almost every way imaginable. The relationship between Cecil and Kathy Klopstock proves to be as barren as their titles suggest. Rather than turning to each other, the aristocratic couple have used their servants to satisfy their sexual appetites. Besides Victor Passerat, several other male secretaries, the handyman, and the assistant chef have all ministered to both the Baron and the Baroness, who has also been attracted to Heloise. In reviewing the list of potential candidates for the fatherhood of Heloise's child, Lister says, "Now, if the Baroness could have been the father in the course of nature she might have been, but the Baron, no" (*ND*, 96–97). Reinforcing the book's Gothic atmosphere, deviation seems to be the norm rather than the exception. Whatever the preference, ravenous promiscuity prevails.

In the brief time during which we see the Baron and Baroness before they entomb themselves in the library, they seem equally callous. As he maneuvers his great car up the long driveway, the Baron almost hits one of the servants. And after pleasantly chatting with the new porter about how well he and his wife appear to be adjusting to his assignment, the Baroness tells Lister to fire the porter since she wants his cabin for one of her cousins. Although Spark provides quick, sharp sketches of the Baron and Baroness, the two aristocrats assume a ghostly aura since one finds many references to their deaths even before they appear in the novel. As Lister says, "They haunt the house . . . like insubstantial bodies, while still alive. . . . My mind floats about, catching at phantoms" (*ND*, 27). Again reminiscent of Murdoch's novel, the next morning three dead bodies are carried out of the large house as Lister's macabre plot reaches its grim denouement.

In *The Unicorn* various characters were locked into obsessive relationships in which one partner often influenced the other like a demon. Although in *Not to Disturb* several characters also seem to be "fixed" in static relationships, Spark emphasizes the mechanical nature of the coupling to such a degree that the individuals frequently resemble automatons instead of human beings. The rigidity of some of the relationships parallels the cold, mechanical ways in which these characters exploit the suffering of others. And in one sense this mechanical indifference proves to be even more horrifying than the passion and terror in Murdoch because it reminds one so vividly of the world outside the novel.

Two of the secretaries, Mr. McGuire with his tape recorder and Mr. Samuel with his movie camera, become extensions of the machines they work so efficiently. Although Mr. McGuire at first represents a flaw in Lister's grand design because Lister didn't expect him to call that evening, the shrewd butler soon incorporates McGuire into his process of "effectively organizing chaos" (*ND*, 55). Mr. McGuire and Mr. Samuel serve as the audiovisual aids used in documenting the evening's events. While Mr. Samuel's camera whines, Mr. McGuire's bobbins whirl (*ND*, 71, 92, 111).

Although the technicians arrive at the chateau at different times, the "Messrs McGuire and Samuel" (*ND*, 79) become almost inseparable. While he is dictating the early morning strategy, Lister also hints at perhaps even a closer connection when he says that at eight o'clock "Mr. Samuel and Mr. McGuire [S & M?] will be in bed" (*ND*, 80). The mechanical nature of their association reinforces the rigid way in which the servants adhere to Lister's plan. If the tape recorder and camera function as the tools of Mr. McGuire and Mr. Samuel, then Messrs McGuire and Samuel function as the tools of the butler: "Lister raises a finger and the discs of the machine begin to spin. . . . Lister raises a finger and the machine stops" (ND, 64). One reader has incisively commented, "At [Lister's] behest men and women behave like clockwork; it seems the only way to behave. Their unrelenting self interest is an aspect of their mechanization, eerily real, eerily unreal."[7]

Just as Calvin Blick in *The Flight from the Enchanter,* Jamesie in *The Unicorn,* and Annabel's determined press agent in *The Public Image* tried to use the camera to freeze contingent reality into a fixed form, so do Mr. Samuel and Lister try to capture their distorted vision of reality by means of photography. While Lister poses with his arm around Pablo, he tells him to look inconsolable by thinking of "some disconsolate idea such as your being in Victor Passerat's shoes." Unfortunately one of their portraits of grief will have to be discarded since the brainless handyman "smiled the second time" (ND, 57). In another scene Lister holds a visiting clergyman's warm drink suspended in air. As the doddering minister stretches out his hand to receive it, "The camera clicks smoothly upon the gesture of benediction. Then the Reverend gets his hot toddy" (ND, 62). In still another scene Pablo and Hadrian's attempt to restrain the lusty lunatic on his rampage to the wedding altar is turned into a snapshot of conventional stag party revels. Jonathan Rabin says of this latter photograph: "It's an acid parody of the activities of art in its encounters with the world; as the dregs and the dross get tarted up, forced into codified molds from where they can radiate a dull, familiar meaning."[8] Although many of the photographs in *Not to Disturb* have their zany quality, the shaping of reality to fit a rigid form becomes somewhat frightening. The servants after all have distorted the tragic fact of the slaughter of three people to a narrow-minded vision of their new economic security. This obsessive distortion of vision, suggested by the photography imagery, can be considered demonic in that changeable reality is forced into a coffin of formal stasis.

Just as Mr. McGuire becomes a tape recorder and Mr. Samuel a camera, Lister himself is associated with a machine at least sixteen times. The butler is identified with the telephone, which he operates very efficiently:

> Lister goes to the house-phone, lifts the receiver, and presses a button. He waits. He presses again, leaving his finger on it for some minutes. At last comes a windy answer. (ND, 65)

Although "the phone crackles amok" from the lightning, Lister's telephone becomes the tool through which he attempts to impose order on the various contingent elements that threaten his plot and that are suggested by the storm. A "buzz on the house-telephone" warns Lister of the surprise visit from the Reverend, who before long is cast in an important role in Lister's drama. When the film company from the United States calls, Lister complains, "They should have telephoned yesterday" (*ND*, 79). Finally, when three people die violently in the library, "Lister now telephones to the discreet and well-appointed flat in Geneva which he prudently maintains and extends a welcome to four journalists who have been waiting up all night for the call" (*ND*, 109).

Lister's efficient use of the telephone exemplifies his systematic mind that in many ways seems more mechanical than the machine he operates. Spark supports this analogy by attributing almost human characteristics to the telephone, which as a result of the storm "wheezes," "whistles briefly," "hisses . . . through its wind-pipe," as well as emits "brief gusty sighs," a "bronchial story," and even a "garrulous sirocco" (*ND*, 19–20, 76, 77, 81). All the time "Lister at the phone listens on" (*ND*, 77).

Lister's post at the phone symbolizes his obsessive concern with the details of a plot that climaxes in murder and suicide. Although the butler can be witty and ironic, his fixation with this bloody scheme makes him satanic. Furthermore, all of the telephone wires, camera equipment, and tape recorders with their "dangling" apparatus (*ND*, 111) and "long snaky cords" (*ND*, 51) begin to resemble serpents writhing about in a mechanical hell.

The underworld imagery continues with the cook, who might as well be stoking the fires of Hades as the flame in his oven. Clovis proves to be as ruthless as any of the other servants. He too will feed off the death of his employers since he hopes to profit immeasurably from their catastrophe, which will release him from a job he does not especially relish. When one of the servants asks him about the evening meal, for instance, he snaps, "Cook your own damned dinner" (*ND*, 15). When he is finally coaxed into preparing the meal, he too becomes a master of efficiency who operates with great dexterity and skill:

> Clovis . . . goes across to the large white complicated cooking stove, studies the regulator, turns the dial, opens the stove door, and while looking inside, with the other hand snaps his finger. Heloise runs with a cloth and a spoon and places them in Clovis's hand. Protecting his hand with the cloth, Clovis partly pulls out a casserole dish. He hooks up the lid with the handle of the spoon, peers in, sniffs, replaces the lid, shoves the dish back and closes the oven door. Again, he turns the dial of the regulator. Then with the spoon-handle, he lifts the lids from the two pots which are simmering on top of the stove. He glances inside each and replaces the lids. (*ND*, 15–16)

Clovis knows exactly how long to wait until the dish is cooked, just as he and Lister must know how long to wait before the concoction simmering in the library is "ready." His snapping fingers suggest how easily he turns other people into mechanical agents to do his bidding, while his protected hand demonstrates how he insulates himself from any real danger or involvement. Later he says, for instance, "We've got nothing to hide. We're innocent" (*ND*, 81). Finally, his "hooking up" the handle of the spoon with the casserole lid reveals his quick sense of invention, which will be helpful in dealing with any contingencies that might interfere with the schedule of events in the library. He soon unhooks the back doorbell, for example, so that the household will not be disturbed by two people who are trying to rescue their friend Victor Passerat.

When Clovis has made his careful calculations, he states:

> Fifteen minutes more for the casserole. In seven minutes you move the pots aside. We sit down at half-past seven if we're lucky and they don't decide to dine before they die. (*ND*, 16)

Thus the lives and deaths of three human beings are discussed in the same breath as dinner schedules and recipes. And Clovis, whose name suggests both a spice and a cleft-footed devil, in one sense is cooking his employers as well as a casserole. The underlying theme of cannibalism is given a grim little twist when Clovis orders the nurse to quell the wealthy idiot in an unusual way: "Bite his finger and keep him quiet . . . Bite his finger . . . or you're fired" (*ND*, 101, 102). Interestingly it is the cook who orders the nurse to bite the rich hand that will eventually feed them all.

When Clovis is not checking matters in the kitchen, he is industriously tending to the business in the library. Just as Messrs McGuire and Samuel seem to meld with the machines they operate so efficiently, Clovis becomes almost inseparable from the finely printed magazine contracts, documents, and papers that will create the most savory result from the brew bubbling away in the library. We read, for instance, that "Clovis is busy with his contract" (*ND*, 5), that Clovis "continues his scrutiny of documents" (*ND*, 5), or that Clovis is "studying the fine print" (*ND*, 6). Invariably if Clovis is mentioned, his papers are mentioned as well. At one point, Lister remarks about the two men in the library, "They have ice. All they need now is the Baroness" (*ND*, 19). Confident that the final ingredient will soon be added, Clovis replies, "Oh, she'll come, don't worry," as he "stacks his papers neatly" (*ND*, 19). His most important paper being the screen story about the Klopstock tragedy, Clovis must "amend his script" (*ND*, 84, 85) whenever fortuitous events upset the plot, just as he must occasionally alter the recipe to create the most flavorful casserole.

When the meal is finally served, Clovis tells the other servants that they must no longer respond if a summons from the library is made. Lister adds, "They're as good as gone to kingdom come. . . . However it is I who decides whether or not we answer any summons, hypothetical or otherwise" (*ND*, 29). Lister's aunt agrees, "It is Lister who decides." In this little exchange the two more intellectual servants sow the seeds for another potential revolt that may arise if Lister takes over as the new baron. Someday Clovis, who has done his paperwork "at the butler's desk" (*ND*, 16), may not agree that it must always be Lister who decides. Thus the author hints at the cyclical nature of the plot. Feeding time must come again and again.

Some of the hungriest servants, who also happen to be the most youthful, are Heloise, the pregnant parlor maid; Pablo, the muscular handyman; and Hadrian, the athletic assistant cook. One of the chief symbols of the sexual chaos in the household, Heloise remains uncertain about the identity of the father of her unborn child (who significantly remains unborn for the duration of the novel). Although the father might be almost any male member of the household as well as one of the guests, Heloise bets on the handyman because, as she explains, "It's day and night with Pablo when he's in the mood. After breakfast, even" (*ND*, 7).

Although superficially charming, the young servants remain brutally insensitive to the tragedy they know will occur in the library. Recalling the departmentalization in one of Hieronymus Bosch's paintings of hell, Spark juxtaposes references to the trio slaughtering one another in the library with a scene where this other trio undulate to rock-and-roll music in the bedroom above. While plump Heloise lolls about on her bed like a drowsy fertility goddess mindlessly tapping to the beat of the record, Pablo and Hadrian, her two attendants in waiting, form the other end of the triangle as they shuffle on either side of the foot of her bed. Their mindlessness is reinforced by their mechanical movements: "First Hadrian, then Pablo, start once more to dance, bobbing and swaying as if blown by a current which fuses out from the beat of the music" (*ND*, 70). As they entertain themselves, their discussion of the Baron's homemade pornographic movies creates some absurd yet hellish images that reinforce the cannibalism motif. While explaining her method of using fairy stories as the basis of these pornographic movies, Heloise says, "Lister and Irene . . . joined in with Red Riding Hood. Lister was terrific as the grandmother when he ate me up. You can see in the film that I had a good time. Then Irene got eaten up by Lister's understudy" (*ND*, 71). Although she refers to the next record selection, Heloise more precisely describes the sexual wilderness entangling the entire household when she says, "Anything goes for me" (*ND*, 72).

As their thoughts finally turn to one of the victims who will be murdered in the room below, only the handyman can muster any sympathy:

> Hadrian stops dancing. "You know what?" he says. "Sorry for Victor Passerat I am not. Neither alive nor dead."
> "Nor me," says Heloise.
> "He had a kind of something," Pablo says, jerking his arms as he rocks. (*ND*, 69)

Such monstrous indifference could be found only in hell.

Two other servants who do not actually reside in the main house nevertheless contribute to the demonic theme. When the wife of the porter complains, "All week in my dreams, I've heard the honking at the gate" (*ND*, 23), one might think of the knocking at the gate in *Macbeth*. Shakespeare's porter says that if a "man were a porter of Hell-gate," he would be constantly opening the door; meanwhile, he admits various sinners, saying: "Knock. Knock. Knock. Who's there in the name of Beelzebub?"[9] In Spark's work the knocking is replaced by the periodic honking at the gate of the Klopstock estate, but like his Shakespearean counterpart, Spark's porter admits the damned into hell.

One of the doomed, of course, is the Baroness, who will soon be shot in the library. After being let in the gate, the Baroness talks to the porter as he stands on the side of the long driveway. As the Baroness blithely chatters away in the heated car, she remains totally indifferent to the discomfort of the numb porter, who shivers in the cold night air, clasps his arms about his sides, and again reminds us of Shakespeare's gatekeeper who remarks, "This place is too cold for hell."

If the porter can be seen as Charon who transports lost souls into the underworld, his wife Clara suggests Cassandra as she prophesies the calamity about to fall on the Klopstock dynasty. Since the porter does not reside in the central mansion and has been kept outside Lister's plot, his wife has no way of knowing about the bloody violence that will transpire in the library that evening. Unlike the other servants in the chateau who see all of the details of Lister's scheme yet—in spite of the carrot juice they drink—remain blind to its essential horror, Clara knows nothing of the particular threads of Lister's grand design yet seems to be the only one who senses that something dreadful will soon take place. She utters, "I can feel it in the air like electricity" (*ND*, 17). Her name suggesting her insight, Clara sees a vision of hell in her "terrible dreams" (*ND*, 107) and knows "something must be happening up there" (*ND*, 22). While the other servants rock and roll as murder is committed, Clara exclaims, "I think I am going mad" (*ND*, 17).

Clara would certainly feel deranged if she had attended the bizarre wedding that Lister organizes to get control of the Klopstock fortune.

Here the butler shapes one contingent element after another so that it fits neatly into his demonic scheme. An unexpected visit from a senile clergyman provides the official stamp for his blasphemous ceremony. Arriving on motorbike in the middle of the night and urging sex-depressant pills on everyone, the Reverend, like the traditional morality he represents, frequently dozes off. His somnolence, however, equips him admirably for his performance in Lister's drama. Heloise's pregnancy, blamed on "him in the attic," supplies the minister with the "just cause" for the ceremony. A bunch of violets from the middle of the funeral wreath serves nicely as the bridal bouquet, while Victor Passerat's white mink coat becomes a lovely bridal dress even though it does not quite reach around the bride's bulging tummy.

The groom meanwhile wears a red jumpsuit, "neighs jubilantly through his large teeth and shakes his long white wavy hair" (ND, 94). Making his marriage seem more like a Witches' Sabbath than a religious occasion, the "zestful cretin" attacks several maidens on his way to the makeshift altar in the parlor. After wriggling out of his jumpsuit, the naked lunatic releases his lust upon the new bride only seconds after she has recited her vows. Seeing an advantage even in this unexpected event, Lister explains: "And so, my dear Heloise, nobody can now contest the validity of your nuptials on the grounds that they haven't been consummated" (ND, 102). The wedding between the zealous maniac and the expanding parlor maid turns a religious ritual into a ludicrous mockery of a sacred union. Instead of being a holy ceremony, this travesty resembles a black mass conducted by the Marx brothers. Although the vision here is colored by the absurd, we are still gazing deeply into the abyss.

Darkening the outlook even more, a phone call at the end of the novel is put through to South America to the Baron's brother, Count Rudolph Klopstock. But even from Rio de Janeiro the only message volleyed back to Switzerland is: "The butler won't fetch Count Klopstock to the phone. Absolutely refuses. He's locked in the study with some friends and he's on no account to be disturbed" (ND, 117–18). Like one of Ted Hughes' desperate poems,[10] Spark's bleak vision spreads out from her hell-house in dizzying circles until it encompasses the entire universe, which also must not be disturbed.

The only temporary relief from the Stygian landscape comes in a rather unusual form. Having escorted Victor Passerat to the Klopstock chateau, his two friends spend most of the remainder of the novel waiting anxiously for him to come out. A male transvestite and a burly masseuse, Alex and Anne could ostensibly be thought of as the novel's odd couple. In fact, for the first half of the book they are referred to as the "two ladies" in the green car waiting for Victor. Their location outside the chateau becomes symbolic, for strange as they may seem,

Passerat's two friends prove to be the only ones who show any compassion for Victor, whom they believe to be in real danger. In the section where Mr. Samuel casually dismisses the couple, we read:

> The masseuse is large but she appears to have very little moral resistance. She starts to cry, with huge baby-sobs, while her companion, Alex, his square bony face framed in a silk head scarf and his eyes pleadingly laden with make-up under finely shaped eyebrows, puts out a bony hand to touch her face. "Come back in the car, Anne" he says, giving Mr. Samuel a look of hurt umbrage. (*ND*, 40)

Ringing the bell, banging their fists on the back door, clamoring on the porch, Alex and Anne represent the humanity that cannot break into Lister's fiendish plot. One by one the other characters refuse to recognize the human element: when he hears about the two women waiting in the car, the Baron mumbles, "Let them wait" (*ND*, 18); after he disconnects the doorbell, Clovis explains, "We need our meal in peace" (*ND*, 28); and even though the knocking continues, "Nobody takes any notice" (*ND*, 104).

Although apparently deviant, Alex and Anne demonstrate a normal, genuine concern for their friend. Yet they are referred to as "those two strange ones" (*ND*, 88) or a "suspicious pair" (*ND*, 108) by the other characters, who although more physically common, have nevertheless engaged in all forms of aberrant behavior. Finally, Alex and Anne symbolize the contingent that must not interfere with Lister's intricate plot. As the moviemaker, Mr. Samuel, says about the couple, "Forget them . . . . They're only extras" (*ND*, 108). Similarly, Lister explains, "They don't come into the story" (*ND*, 38). Spark seems to agree as she removes this unique pair from the novel in an arrogantly expedient manner.

The author's real purpose emerges, however, when one examines her Gothic imagery more closely. Lister's first words are:

> Their life . . . a general mist of error
> Their death, a hideous storm of terror.

Although the butler's opening allusion to *The Duchess of Malfi* foreshadows the violence that will erupt behind the locked library doors later that evening, it also introduces the actual tempest that contributes so much to the novel's Gothic atmosphere. Moving through the entire work, the storm assumes a personality of its own: sometimes it is remote and ominous as when it "has retreated from the near vicinity of the house, but continues to prowl on the lake and the mountain-sides" (*ND*, 104). Other times the storm makes a direct attack as it "beats on the windows and detonates in the park" (*ND*, 96). The storm threatens not only the Klopstock chateau but also the traditional structures of fiction as Spark so playfully manipulates this convention, prompting one critic to call the book a "mock-mod-Gothic" thriller.[11]

Lister is depending on the wind from the storm to bang the outdoor shutters, which he has directed the handyman to loosen. He hopes that this clatter as well as the storm's thunder will muffle any suspicious noises issuing from the Klopstock residence on this fateful night. The storm cooperates with Lister all too well. During the mock wedding scene, when Heloise worries about all the noise from the idiot, Lister assures her that the lunatic's ragings will not be distinguishable from the other discordant sounds of the evening: then "an instant of quick lightning at the windows followed by a grumble of thunder reinforces his argument" (*ND*, 94). The next morning at the exact moment when the Inspector asks if Lister heard any shots during the night, the wind—on cue— "encircles the house and the shutters bang" while Lister explains, "No, Inspector. It was a wild night" (*ND*, 112). Spark's tour de force, however, involves that outrageously efficient lightning bolt:

> which strikes the clump of elms so that the two friends huddled there are killed instantly without pain, zigzags across the lawns, illuminating the lily-pond and the sunken rose garden like a self-stricken flash-photographer, and like a zip-fastener ripped from its garment by a sexual maniac, it is flung slapdash across Lake Leman and back to skim the rooftops of the house, leaving intact . . . the well-insulated telephone wires which Lister, on the telephone to Geneva, has rather feared might break down. (*ND*, 109)

The huddling friends happen to be Alex and Anne, the two contingent elements who have posed the only real threat to Lister's grand design and who in a subordinate clause are now neatly eliminated. But the lightning has not disturbed the lines of communication between Lister and the four journalists to whom he will sell his sordid tale. Spark's obvious exploitation of authorial power parallels Lister's manipulation of form and thus mocks the very notion of fiction—Lister, after all, being a type of novelist himself. Like Murdoch, Spark then may be implying that a truly moral vision is based on a healthy respect for the contingent, which we should not try to mold into some rigid pattern, whether it be a novel or a demonic scheme to profit from violence and bloodshed.

Thus Spark's horrific tale, like Eliot's poem, indirectly expresses its didactic theme by traversing over a moral wasteland. The hellish vision created in both works makes the reader thirst for the cooling waters of human kindness and love, qualities not easily found in the barren territory explored by either novelist or poet. Even though Spark relies upon wit and black humor to guide us through her lurid Swiss chateau, Eliot's line from "The Fire Sermon" not only names the lake outside the chateau but also describes an emotional response that might be evoked by her dark novel:

> By the waters of Leman
> I sat down and wept.

PART III
John Fowles

A ROOM WITHOUT A VIEW
The Collector

In *The Situation of the Novel* Bernard Bergonzi recognizes that along with Iris Murdoch and Muriel Spark, John Fowles has produced fiction "at a considerable distance from the well-made realistic novel as conventionally understood."[1] One might compare, for instance, Spark's playful manipulation of form in *Not to Disturb* with Fowles's experimental techniques in *The French Lieutenant's Woman*, where Fowles questions the arbitrary power of the author not by imposing one obviously artificial pattern but rather by refusing to lay down any rigid structure at all and instead providing multiple endings that more directly involve the reader in the art of fiction. This technique reinforces the central theme of freedom as Sarah Woodruff becomes a type of didactic demon who haunts the Victorian mind of Charles Smithson and teaches him to look at the world with a more modern existential awareness.

One of Fowles's earlier novels, however, serves as a clearer example of demonic didacticism due to its bizarre subject matter and decidedly moral foundation. In many ways *The Collector* crystallizes some of the main themes explored by both Murdoch and Spark. Certainly the book's didactic intentions were noticed by the reviewer who said, "as a novel that is trying to make a serious moral statement and making it seriously and well, *The Collector* deserves attention."[2] The very title of Fowles's first novel points to the central evil of "collecting" or capturing what is free by imposing a rigid structure upon its contingent reality. In fact, John Ditsky has written about *The French Lieutenant's Woman, The Magus,* and *The Collector*: "The act of capture, especially in the chess sense, pervades all three works, providing a distinctively English chill that we may recognize from the work of . . . Murdoch or Spark."[3] In all three writers the imprisonment often results from some type of demonic obsession. Mischa Fox collected various creatures and enslaved them in states of servile dependency while Martin Lynch-Gibbon confined Georgie Hands in a clandestine apartment that seemed like a "subterranean place, remote, enclosed, hidden"[4] (a perfect description of the underground cell in *The Collector*). Hannah Crean-Smith was trapped in her room at Gaze Castle and the characters of Peckham Rye were frozen into mechanical relationships. Finally, Annabel Christopher was caught in the snares of her own public image while the servants of the Klopstock chateau bottled up their masters in the fateful library after virtually hanging a sign on the door that read "Not to Disturb."

In *The Collector* the imprisonment theme assumes its most literal significance as a shy butterfly enthusiast gradually decides to capture a form of beauty that is distinctly human. In this novel about a man who locks up a girl in his secret cellar, point of view is directly related to the central theme. The story is revealed first as the pale entomologist tells it, then as the lovely girl privately records it in her diary. The fact that the same story is told twice by the novel's two main characters emphasizes the distance between them. This two-part structure reinforces the novel's compartmental quality: each of the characters is caught in his own cell of limited perspective. While in *The Unicorn* two observers related the central tale, here two people directly involved in the plot tell their own stories. It's as if Gerald Scottow and Hannah Crean-Smith had become the narrators of *The Unicorn*. The jailer and prisoner both tell their own tales. The difference in style adds to the tension: the entomologist named Frederick Clegg is factual, methodical, and prosaic while his more erratic captive named Miranda Grey can be fiery, lyrical, or philosophical. The static-kinetic polarities of style support the theme as the fixed will of the collector presses inexorably against the fluttering protests of the emotional young girl. The two viewpoints also inversely emphasize the Murdochian concept of attention or "seeing" the otherness of individuals. The two separate versions suggest that the necessary moral vision between the two characters remains blurred. When in *A Severed Head* Murdoch allowed Martin Lynch-Gibbon to tell his own story, the reader could trace a certain moral development in the narrator. In *The Collector* Clegg does not really mature or grow in any way, and although Miranda changes, her growth is not allowed to come to fruition. In Miranda's tale especially, Fowles writes a type of frustrated Bildungsroman.

Although the point of view is presented subjectively by two participants rather than two "outside" observers as in *The Unicorn*, Frederick Clegg must be considered a "participant" who actually remains an observer. Just as he looks at butterflies, catches them, and then continues to look at them after they have been mounted in glass cases, so does he watch a beautiful art student in London for about two years before he finally decides to encase her in a hidden basement room of an ancient rural cottage he has recently purchased. Winning a football pool gives him the power to change his demonic fantasy into lurid reality. Even after he imprisons his prized possession, he does not interact with her on a human level but continues to observe her just as he passively gazes at his butterflies in their glass cases.

The comparison between girl and butterfly becomes one of the dominant motifs in the book. Before he has even kidnapped Miranda, Clegg says: "Seeing her always made me feel like I was catching a rarity, going up to it very careful, heart-in-mouth as they say. A Pale Clouded Yellow, for instance."[5] Clegg could observe Miranda every day after she had come home from boarding school because her house stood opposite the Town Hall Annexe where he worked. Although she "didn't look once" at him, he "watched the back of her head and her hair in a long pigtail. It was very pale, silky, like Burnet cocoons" (C, 3). He admits that he grows so intrigued with her appearance that in "the evening I marked it in my observation diary, at first with X, and then when I knew her name with M" (C, 3). But his obsession remains cold and dispassionate. One critic has said, "One of the horrifying things about this horrifying little man is the matter-of-fact way in which he conceives, carries out, and writes about his crime. He does not gloat; although sexually disordered and a voyeur, he is not a sadist; he is merely obdurate and without pity or remorse."[6] His scientific manner replicates Lister's methodical yet diabolic scheming in Spark's novel. On the night Clegg abducts Miranda in his van, he comments, "It was like catching the Mazarine Blue again or a Queen of Spain Fritillary" (C, 28). Later when Miranda begs him "very gently and nicely" to release her, Clegg manages to resist by again comparing the delicacy of the situation to his previous entomological adventures: "It was like not having a net and catching a specimen you wanted in your first and second fingers . . . you had to nip the thorax, and it would be quivering there" (C, 39). The butterfly imagery that supports the role of Clegg as a type of mad scientist continues. But even more sinister implications are revealed when Miranda changes her hairstyle and applies makeup after her bath: "Sophisticated, that's exactly the word. Of course, she made me feel all clumsy and awkward. I had the same feeling I did when I had watched an imago emerge, and then to have to kill it. I mean, the beauty confuses you, you don't know what you want to do any more" (C,84). But any gesture he makes will reflect his reaction to an insect, not a human being.

While Clegg sees nothing particularly immoral in collecting either butterflies or girls, Miranda immediately becomes aware of the moral implications in the similarity between herself and Clegg's butterflies whom she refers to as "my fellow-victims" (C, 54, 135). She even tries to make the parallel more explicit for Clegg, who agrees that he has collected her "in a manner of speaking." Miranda argues: "No, not in a manner of speaking. Literally. You've pinned me in this little room and you can come and gloat over me" (C, 42). Ironically, one evening during a game of charades, Clegg cannot guess that the word Miranda acts out is "butterfly" (C, 87). Miranda also comes to realize that the scientist will not interact emotionally with his specimen but will always remain an observer: "I could scream abuse at him all day long; he wouldn't mind at all. It's me he wants, my look, my outside; not my emotions or my mind or my soul or even my body. Not anything *human*. He's a collector. That's the great dead thing in him" (C, 171). In one of her most desperate yet insightful moments Miranda, the artist, paints the painfully vivid finishing touches upon the butterfly pattern:

> I am one in a row of specimens. It's when I try to flutter out of line that he hates me. I'm meant to be dead, pinned, always the same, always beautiful. . . .
> He is solid; immovable, iron-willed. He showed me one day what he called his killing bottle. I'm imprisoned in it. Fluttering against the glass. Because I can see through it I still think I can escape. I have hope. But it's all an illusion.
> A thick round wall of glass. (C, 217–18)

As Clegg relates his experience of pinning down Miranda behind this glass wall, he paradoxically becomes an "involved" first-person narrator who never really participates in the action in a human way but remains an observer or a collector until the very end.

Karen Lever has written: "The collector mentality is Fowles's constant target. The collector is interested in things and people for the wrong reasons: he has the desire to classify them, to kill their individuality by seeing only that aspect of them that fits his categorizing scheme, and he wants to possess them as objects. For Fowles, the scientist at his worst is a collector."[7] Echoing Iris Murdoch and Elias Canetti, Fowles writes in an article on conservation: "One can safely assume that anyone who still collects (i.e., kills) some field of living life just for pleasure and vanity has all the makings of a concentration-camp commandant."[8] It is not surprising that Clegg talks of Gestapo tactics when he keeps all the newspapers and radios away from the sample of life he has collected.

Another hobby that further defines Clegg's role as a collector and observer is his interest in photography. As we have seen, this particular pastime has been cultivated by several characters in Murdoch and Spark, all of whom tried to encase fluid reality within a fixed form, which further suggested the static nature of their obsession. Calvin Blick used the "dirty" photograph of Rosa for blackmail; Annabel Christopher wanted the "happy" photographs of herself and her husband for her public image; Lister took the "sad" photographs of the mourners for the movie magazines; and Jamesie Evercreech collected "unusual" photographs of Gerald Scottow to feed his private fantasies. Clegg's pornographic photographs can most easily be compared to Jamesie's. For both men the photographs serve as a way to control the reality they can not manage outside the frame of a camera. The impotent Frederick Clegg gains power by observing the photographs he took of Miranda on the day he chloroformed her: "I could take my time with them. They didn't talk back at me" (*C*, 109). He gets ideas for his snapshots by looking at pornographic magazines, one of which, called *Shoes*, displays "very interesting pictures of girls, mainly their legs, wearing different sorts of shoes, some just shoes and belts, they were really unusual pictures, artistic" (*C*, 114). The example makes explicit the fragmentation and dehumanization involved in pornography, which specializes in body parts rather than complete human beings. As Miranda's older friend points out, art tries to create the essence of life through the imagination, while photography, the antithesis of art, merely reproduces life in a mechanical way and thus often kills it. Clegg seems most obsessively determined to kill life in the scene after Miranda attempts to make love to him and he ultimately responds by controlling her with the only instrument he knows how to use—his camera. After tying her to the bed, Clegg explains:

> I got her garments off and at first she wouldn't do as I said but in the end she lay and stood like I ordered (I refused to take if she did not co-operate). So I got my pictures. I took her till I had no more bulbs left. (*C*, 117–18)

Thus Clegg "takes" Miranda with a machine. The camera here suggests a sexual instrument that the impotent entomologist uses to rape his beautiful specimen. William J. Palmer supports such an explicitly sexual reading by referring to a dramatic adaptation of *The Collector* that played in London in 1971 and 1972 and conveyed Fowles's meaning in a degrading episode:

> As Clegg began to shoot, a brutal strobe light pierced the dimness of the stage and began rhythmically faster and faster and harder and harder to assault with pounding shafts of light the tableau of Miranda tied to the bed while Clegg prowled the shadows excitedly caressing his camera. Finally, the scene, and the audience, dropped into exhausted darkness. The mechanical orgasm had been attained and what had approximated a human world had been transformed into an eerie, oppressive, fragmented world of unnatural light and sinister shadows. The whole dramatic experience left an unhealthy taste in the mouth of the audience.[9]

One of the novel's darkest moments occurs when Clegg says, "I got the pictures developed and printed that night. The best ones were with her face cut off" (C, 118). Without a head, Miranda cannot even look back at this demonic observer who can now freely focus upon the body parts that have become his obsession. This photographic decapitation of Miranda forms a grim counterpoint to the scene where she actually has the chance to use an ax on Clegg but at the final second cannot kill another human being, even though she knows her restraint may cost her own life.

Besides the imprisonment and photography motifs, metaphors of hell fall like shadows over the literature of all three novelists. In Murdoch's *A Severed Head* Martin Lynch-Gibbon is obsessed with Honor Klein, whose image looms "vast across his way as the horizon itself or the spread wings of Satan" (*SH*, 150). In Spark's *The Ballad of Peckham Rye* Douglas Dougal maintains that the bumps on his head indicate where his horns had been sawed off by a surgeon. Meanwhile the diabolic servants in *Not to Disturb* transform the Klopstock chateau into a hell-house. For Miranda also the dark, damp cellar surrounded by layers of rock and enclosed by thick iron doors soon resembles a chamber in hell. Feeling suffocated by the stifling atmosphere and the maddeningly ordinary quality of her jailer, the young art student one day writes:

> It's afternoon. I should be in life class. Does the world go on? Does the sun still shine? Last night, I thought—I am dead. This is death. This is hell. There wouldn't be other people in hell. Or just one, like him. The devil wouldn't be devilish and rather attractive, but like him. (*C*, 131)

Almost a week later the futility of her situation sinks further down upon her: "Today I've been thinking he could keep me here forever. It wouldn't be very long, because I'd die. It's absurd, it's diabolical—but there is no way of escape" (*C*, 159). Four days later she again compares her captor to Satan because he continually tempts her with candy, flowers, and caviar: "I know he's the Devil showing me the world that can be mine. So I don't sell myself to him. I cost him a lot in little things, but I know he wants me to ask for something big. He's dying to make me grateful. But he shan't" (*C*, 180–81). Finally when Clegg allows Miranda, who has feigned appendicitis, to rush through the two heavy open doors, only to find her supposedly alarmed captor waiting outside with a hammer, she says:

> Another escape. So nearly, it seemed at one point. But it never was. He's a devil. (*C*, 216)

Although Miranda's basement becomes a room in hell, it also assumes positive aspects, as did the wine cellar in which Martin Lynch-Gibbon attacked Honor Klein. In both cases the basement suggests the descent into the underworld of the self, which can ultimately lead to a more profound knowledge of one's inner being. Ironically, the ancient cellar in which Clegg locks Miranda is reputed to have been originally built as a secret chapel.

Besides the underground prison, ghastly photography sessions, and Satanic imagery, Fowles supports the novel's Gothic atmosphere with the cornerstone of suspense. Even though many of the events are narrated twice, certain information is often withheld during the first telling. And the terrible outcome remains unknown until the very last part of the novel when the demonic collector takes over once again as narrator. Miranda's various attempts to escape are told forcefully by both Clegg and the girl. Much of the book's energy is derived from its carefully worked out details. Miranda's efforts to dig a tunnel with a long nail she has found, for instance, clearly convey the futility of her situation. As Granville Hicks has said, "The pains Fowles has taken to make the abduction and imprisonment credible are impressive: there is very little indeed that the reader has to take on faith."[10] Clegg's graphic description of Miranda's illness seems both realistic and grotesque: "She said she couldn't breathe, and then she brought up a mass of phlegm. It was a funny dark brown, I didn't like the look of it at all" (C, 287). Roy Newquist has remarked, "The horror grew as the story progressed, but no matter how nightmarish it became, it was still believable."[11]

Although point of view, plot, and imagery are skillfully employed, much of the richness of Fowles's work springs from his complex characterization, a feature that perhaps explains some of the diverse critical reactions to each of his two principal figures.[12] Here his aesthetic strategy parallels his theme. Just as he shows the evil of "collecting" other people in narrow cells, either real or imagined, so does he refrain from placing his characters into a mold that would inevitably lead to only one rigid interpretation. Fowles refuses to lock either Clegg or Miranda into the cell of a purely one-dimensional characterization: he will not encase their fluid personalities into one fixed photograph.

Although Clegg does seem obsessed in a demonic way with the physical attributes of Miranda, Fowles tries to demonstrate, for instance, that his protagonist's unfortunate childhood and lack of education kindled his neurosis. Since his father had been killed in an automobile accident when the boy was only two and his promiscuous mother soon abandoned him, Clegg was raised in a mean lower-class environment by his relatives. Although his Uncle Dick cared for him and took him fishing, before too long he had a stroke, died, and removed the masculine influence suggested by his name from young Frederick's life. The youth was therefore left at the mercy of his narrow-minded, repressive Aunt Annie, who hated both dust and "vulgar women."

Thus even though Clegg victimizes Miranda, he suffers himself. After he wins all the money, he remains imprisoned in the category of "lower class." At the expensive hotel where he takes his aunt and cousin, he senses that the hotel people "still treated me behind the scenes for what I was—a clerk. It was no good throwing money around. As soon as we spoke or did something we gave the game away" (*C*, 8). At a "posh restaurant" Clegg explains "how everything in the room seemed to look down at us" (*C*, 9). Clegg concludes, "If you ask me, London's all arranged for the people who can act like public school boys" (*C*, 9). Even when he purchases and renovates his rural cottage, the various realtors and tradespeople become aware of his lower-class background and take advantage of him: as he says, "everyone fleeced me" (*C*, 18).

While Clegg usually remains the observer in his relationship with Miranda, he is often ridiculed in his daily contacts with the impetuous art student. In most cases, however, he tries to hide his embarrassment and avoid conflict. And although Miranda is jailed in a narrow cell by Clegg, she frequently tries to imprison him in some rigid category. One moment she writes, "He's what people call a 'nice young man.'" Later she compares him to "a male assistant in a draper's." Almost a scientist herself, she adds, "Absolutely sexless (he looks)" (*C*, 128). The most vivid example of Miranda's tendency to classify Clegg evolves from the novel's allusions to *The Tempest*. Frederick at first tells Miranda his name is Ferdinand, which he thinks sounds more exotic than Frederick. But rather than think of her captor as Shakespeare's handsome young prince, Miranda sees a closer resemblance to the play's monster and so refers to Clegg as Caliban throughout her diary. Clegg, of course, has been psychologically deformed by society, but Miranda exacerbates the situation by calling attention to his beastly rather than his human nature.

Another paradox involves the master-slave aspect of the relationship between Miranda and Clegg. Although Miranda's ultimate freedom is restricted by Clegg, she often reverses the situation as she treats him like an obedient servant: "He has a way of standing with his hands by his side or behind his back, as if he doesn't know what on earth to do with them. Respectfully waiting for me to give my orders" (*C*, 128). Elsewhere Clegg himself admits, "Sometimes she made me go away as soon as supper was over" (*C*, 65). In one scene Miranda virtually turns Clegg into an automaton for her own amusement:

> Today at lunch I wanted the Worcester sauce. He hardly ever forgets to bring anything I might want. But no Worcester sauce. So he gets up, goes out, undoes the padlock holding the door open, locks the door, gets the sauce in the outer cellar, unlocks the door, repadlocks it, comes back. And then looks surprised when I laugh. (*C*, 147)

The characters' roles do then occasionally reverse, and Clegg some-times senses that Miranda looks at him as if he were a creature being observed in a laboratory. In one episode Miranda calls Clegg a perfect "specimen" of "petit bourgeois squareness" (*C*, 78). Elsewhere she bar-gains, "If you let me go, I should want to see you, because you interest me very much." Aware of the possible detachment in her "interest," Clegg then asks, "Like you go to the zoo?" (*C*, 73). Still another time Clegg compares himself to an extraterrestrial visitor: "The way she was looking at me really made me sick. As if I wasn't human hardly. Not a sneer. Just as if I was something out of outer space. Fascinating almost" (*C*, 90).

In light of Clegg's reactions here and Miranda's namecalling it is difficult to understand why one critic maintains that Fowles considers Miranda an "exemplar" of superior values.[13] In fact, the author himself has written in *The Aristos* that even though Miranda had the potential to become something better, she cannot be thought of as perfect: "Far from it—she was . . . a prig, a liberal-humanist snob, like so many university students."[14] Miranda, for example, often seems to pin Clegg with a lower-class label by attacking his language, which in England can be a good indicator of an individual's background and education. One day Miranda asks him, "You know how rain takes the color out of every-thing? That's what you do to the English language. You blur it every time you open your mouth" (*C*, 69). Later she complains about his perpetual use of clichés. Miranda also frequently assails Clegg for his total lack of cultural knowledge and aesthetic sensibility, two more barometers of an individual's social class. When, on a tour upstairs, she sees porcelain wild ducks on a "lovely old fireplace," she insanely smashes them on the hearth, explaining that "ugly ornaments don't deserve to exist" (*C*, 137). His meekness, his hackneyed phrases, and his bad taste all cause Miranda to proclaim very categorically that Clegg "is absolutely inferior to me in all ways" (*C*, 238). She asks, "How could I ever look in any way but down on him?" (*C*, 251). She even assigns Clegg to the class she derisively calls New People, which describes those who have recently acquired money but not the intelligence or aesthetic sensibility to go with it.

Of course, Miranda is superior to Clegg in many ways, but Fowles writes in *The Aristos* that the proper attitude of the intellectually gifted to the less talented depends upon a sense of responsibility, not arrogance. Fowles also makes clear, however, that Miranda becomes more responsi-ble. She does change, especially in her attitude toward other people. Ironically, her growth comes largely as a result of her incarceration by the demonic collector.

One of the lessons Miranda learns through her frustrating experience with Clegg involves her relationship with her mother. Just as Clegg has collected Miranda and stuffed her into a narrow room, so has she emotionally pigeonholed her parent. Miranda writes, "She's always been my mother I've hated or been ashamed of" (*C,* 151). Even Clegg had mentioned Mrs. Grey's "la-di-da" manner and her drinking. When Miranda recounts a conversation with Clegg about her parents, she explains: "I talked . . . about D and M, in a bright little matter-of-fact voice. He knew about M. I suppose the whole town knows" (*C,* 127). Her very phrase "he knew about M" reinforces the idea that Miranda feels that there exists only one category or slot in which to place her mother, only one nasty label to pin on her. As a result of her recent suffering, however, Miranda gradually understands that she never really thought of her mother as a complex "other" person but only as an "ambitious middle-class bitch" (*C,* 59). Realizing she has never offered her mother enough sympathy, Miranda writes:

> I haven't given her this last year . . . one half of the consideration I've given the beastly creature upstairs just this last week. I feel that I could overwhelm her with love now. Because I haven't felt so sorry for her for years. I've always excused myself—I've said I'm kind and tolerant with everyone else, she's the one person I can't be like that with, and there has to be an exception to the general rule. So it doesn't matter. But of course that's wrong. She's the last person that should be an exception to the general rule. (*C,* 151)

The passage illustrates Miranda's growing compassion. Because of her confinement she has been forced to engage in a type of dialogue with herself, analyzing what "excuses" one aspect of her personality has made and then criticizing those excuses with a more generous nature. This educational process has evolved because of her imprisonment by "that beastly creature upstairs," who unintentionally has thus become a didactic demon.

A considerable amount of Miranda's diary is devoted to her relationship with an older artist referred to as G.P., and here also her imprisonment at the hands of Clegg teaches her to be much more tolerant and understanding. Right from the start she had been deeply influenced by G.P.'s stringently unconventional mode of living, his passionate dedication to art, and even his brutal honesty. His abrasive criticism of her own paintings at first inflicted much pain but ultimately led to her total respect for his judgment. G.P. seems to epitomize one of "The Few" whom Fowles describes as that limited number of ethically and intellectually superior individuals who must lead and teach "The Many" other members of society for their own betterment. Of course, as Fowles explains in his philosophical notes, the dividing line between The

Few and The Many usually runs within each individual and not just between individuals.[15] But to some critics' consternation, Fowles makes it clear that G.P. exemplifies The Few far more than The Many.[16]

His emotional honesty especially appeals to Miranda. When Miranda's friend Piers insolently cleans wax out of his ears while listening to Bach on G.P.'s stereo, Miranda recalls the artist's volatile reaction that she describes as being:

> wonderfully terrible, because passion is something you never see. I've grown up among people who've tried to hide passion. He was raw. Naked. Trembling with rage. (C, 178)

In a world where too many people opt for complacency, comfort, mediocrity, G.P. forms a citadel of value for Miranda, who at times believes she is falling in love with him. Her chief reservation results from her own tendency to be a type of collector, for although she admires him, she has placed G.P. into the category of "older man." In another entry in her diary she writes: "I know exactly the sort of person I want to marry, someone with a mind like G.P.'s, only much nearer my own age, and with the looks I like" (C, 150). Her fragmented specifications vaguely resemble a list one might make at a used car lot: keep the engine; get rid of the body. Elsewhere her sense of perfection causes her to try to move G.P. from one category to another as if he were a butterfly who could be put into a more attractive display case: Miranda unrealistically writes, "If I had a fairy godmother—please, make G.P. twenty years younger. And please, make him physically attractive to me" (C, 153). Several weeks after that entry Miranda begins to recognize an aspect of her own selfish nature and inexperience when she reflects upon Jane Austen's Emma, who also had rather rigid specifications for anyone wanting to be her husband. Miranda then wonders, "is G.P. Mr. Knightley? . . . Of course G.P. has lived a life and has views that would make Mr. Knightley turn in his grave. But Mr. Knightley could never have been a phoney. Because he was a hater of pretence, selfishness, snobbism" (C, 235). Finally, a month later, Miranda's perception blossoms with a new sensitivity and awareness as she realizes that G.P. is the most important person she has ever met and if released, she would go to him:

> I still can't say I love him. But now I begin to see that it's because I don't know what love is. I'm Emma with her silly little clever-clever theories of love and marriage, and love is something that comes in different clothes, with a different face, and perhaps it takes a long time for you to accept it, to be able to call it love. (C, 257)

Her reluctance to continue to categorize and "collect" people and emotions into tidy compartments gives her new strength: "Perhaps he would be dry and cold when it came to it. Say I'm too young, he wasn't ever really serious, and—a thousand things. But I'm not afraid. I would risk it" (*C*, 257). Once again valuable lessons are learned in that hellish basement room.

In addition to changing her attitude toward her mother and G.P., Miranda begins to look at Clegg differently. Certain passages seem to represent a breakthrough in the barriers erected between Miranda and her collector. Miranda says at one point: "It's weird. Uncanny. But there is a sort of relationship between us." She then describes how they "slip into teasing states that are almost friendly." She explains how part of her wants to get Clegg off guard and part of her simply remains lonely. But she also acknowledges a "mysterious part" she can't define:

> Perhaps it's just knowledge. Just knowing a lot about him. And knowing someone automatically makes you feel close to him. Even when you wish he was on another planet. . . .
> It is not that I have forgotten what other people are like. But other people seem to have lost reality. The only real person in my world is Caliban.
> It can't be understood. It just is. (*C*, 148)

In spite of herself she reacts to Clegg on a human level. The "knowledge" she speaks of sounds similar to what Iris Murdoch calls the necessary "attention" or awareness we must have for the otherness of fellow human beings.

Conscious that she is becoming more sensitive and wise, Miranda writes, "I'm growing up so quickly down here. Like a mushroom. Or is it that I've lost my sense of balance? Perhaps it's all a dream" (*C*, 165). Despite her qualifications Miranda's personality is expanding. And in one scene after she has criticized Clegg, she shares a poignant moment with her captor. To apologize for her rudeness, she tells an imaginary story about a princess locked in a dungeon by an ugly monster. The princess promises the monster that he will no longer be ugly if he only frees her. The monster grants her wish and is turned into a handsome nobleman who marries the princess. After her lengthy monologue Miranda says to Clegg:

> Now it's your turn to tell a fairy story.
> He just said, I love you.
> And yes, he had more dignity than I did then and I felt small, mean. Always sneering at him, jabbing him, hating him and showing it. It was funny, we sat in silence facing each other and I had a feeling I've had once or twice before, of the most peculiar closeness to him—not love or attraction or sympathy in any way. But linked destiny. Like being

shipwrecked on an island—a raft—together. In every way not wanting
to be together. But together. . . .
Just those three words, said and meant. I love you.
They were quite hopeless. He said it as he might have said, I have
cancer.
His fairy story. (*C*, 200)

The passage can be interpreted in a number of ways. Clegg seems aware
that it would indeed be a fanciful tale if an intelligent well-to-do girl like
Miranda would ever fall in love with someone like him. His simple
declaration gains prominence in light of all the stipulations involved in
the story of the princess. But on the other hand, the entire account is
conveyed as Miranda's perception, not Clegg's. One would also have to
point out to Clegg that people do not usually lock up those they love.
Nevertheless the account seems to represent an important stage in
Miranda's growing awareness of Clegg as a unique other individual.

As a result of her changed attitude toward her mother, G.P., and
Clegg, Miranda feels that she has been transformed. Toward the end of
her diary, she writes: "A strange thought: I would not want this not to
have happened. Because if I escape I shall be a completely different and
I think better person. Because if I don't escape, if something dreadful
happened, I shall still know that the person I was and would have stayed
if this hadn't happened was not the person I now want to be. It's like
firing a pot. You have to risk the cracking and the warping" (*C*, 270). Her
last two sentences seem to express the theme of demonic didacticism:
through her hellish experience with Clegg she has learned invaluable
lessons. But unfortunately the utensil is cracked in the firing.

Although Miranda gains new knowledge, she never has the chance to
apply that knowledge in the world outside her hell-room. Until the very
end Clegg continues to make comments such as: "I liked having her on a
bit" (*C*, 100). And perhaps Miranda most accurately analyzes the way in
which Clegg appreciates her when she writes: "He knows that part of my
beauty is being alive, but it's the dead me he wants. He wants me living-
but-dead. I felt it terribly strong today. That my being alive and changing and having a separate mind and having moods and all that was
becoming a nuisance" (*C*, 218). Miranda understands that what Clegg
really loves is the dead specimen, the static photograph, the fragmented
and manageable work of pornography. Perhaps the only significant
change that has taken place in Clegg depends upon Miranda's perception of the real evil in his nature: "He starts by being a nice little clerk
ends up as a drooling horror-film monster" (*C*, 217).

Clegg does indeed sound quite fiendish when he says to himself just
before his nasty camera-work:

I walked about upstairs, I went and looked at her room, it made me really laugh to think of her down there, she was the one who was going to stay below in all senses and even if it wasn't what she deserved in the beginning she had made it so that she did now. I had real reasons to teach her what was what (C, 114).

His comments cast a lurid glow on the idea of demonic didacticism: the monster does "teach" Miranda "what was what," but the lesson does not turn out to be the one he intended. He wants to train her to serve as a perfect sexual object for his sleazy pornographic pictures, but she begins to bloom into a much more compassionate human being. And one of the symbols Fowles adopts to show Miranda's potential yet ultimately frustrated development is the mirror.

While in *The Flight from the Enchanter* and *The Unicorn* Iris Murdoch turned to this device to suggest the dangers of fantasy and self-absorption, Miranda's looking glass provides a key to understanding her own existential reality:

> Something I have been doing a lot these last days. Staring at myself in the mirror. . . . I try to see what my eyes say. What I am. Why I'm here. . . .
> Anyone who has been locked away like this would understand. You become very real to yourself in a strange way. As you never were before. So much of you is given to ordinary people, suppressed, in ordinary life. (C, 242)

Aware of the dangers of neurotic self-absorption in the Murdochian sense, she admits, "Sometimes it's like a sort of spell, and I have to put my tongue out and wrinkle my nose to break it" (C, 242).

In most cases, however, the looking glass helps Miranda appraise her own situation more objectively:

> I looked in the mirror today and I could see it in my eyes. They look much older and younger. . . . I am older because I have learnt, I am younger because a lot of me consisted of things older people had taught me. All the mud of their stale ideas on the shoe of me.
> The new shoe of me. (C, 267)

But if Miranda uses the mirror in constructive ways, Clegg shows that the device has other functions. Perhaps with no other symbol does Fowles demonstrate so clearly that we are really listening to two tales. In a grimly ironic episode after Miranda has been coughing up phlegm in the throes of pneumonia, Clegg picks up the looking glass for an altogether different purpose:

I felt her and she was cold, though her body was still warm. I ran and got a mirror. I knew that was the way and held it over her mouth but there was no mist. She was dead. (*C*, 295)

What had provided Miranda with an avenue to understanding her life becomes in Clegg's hands the gateway to death. Fowles foreshadows this more bizarre use of the mirror by reminding us early in the novel that the device was made of metal rather than glass so that the collector's visitor would not be able to break it and try to kill herself with its sharp edges. Thus in Clegg's mirror the new "shoe" of Miranda's being blurs into a pornographic magazine about footwear.

After his captive dies, Clegg even tries to employ the looking glass in the way Miranda had, but fails miserably: "I thought I was going mad, I kept on looking in the mirror and trying to see it in my face. I had this horrible idea, I was mad, everyone else could see it, only I couldn't" (*C*, 297). And he never does realize his own derangement, for shortly thereafter he begins making plans for a second guest in his slightly damp but comfortable basement room. This time he intends to get someone who will "respect me more. Someone ordinary I could teach" (*C*, 254). Unwittingly the hellish instructor has taught Miranda some important moral lessons; therefore, one becomes all the more disturbed at the fact that this beautiful student dies before she is able to leave the classroom. As this bleak story turns full cycle, it develops a deep pathos for the lost chances of a morally reshaped young woman to fulfill herself and hence looms as a universal metaphor for the triumph of mediocrity and death over refinement and vitality. As a result of this macabre tale that arouses the reader's moral indignation, the author—even more than the protagonist—can be considered the truly didactic demon. In fact, as a young boy, John Fowles himself often spent his time collecting butterflies.

GREEK GOTHIC
The Magus

Although *The Collector* is the first novel John Fowles published, he actually began writing *The Magus* long before he told Frederick Clegg's story. He worked on the longer novel, in fact, throughout most of the 1950s before it was finally released for publication in 1965. Even though the book gained both critical and popular recognition, the author made stylistic changes and treated the sexual material more explicitly in a revised version that appeared in 1977. These facts strongly suggest that *The Magus* occupies a central position in the Fowles canon.

Widely different from each other in setting and tone, Fowles's novels nevertheless usually involve the education of a protagonist who must embark on some type of journey in order to gain new perspectives and understanding. Miranda Grey learns valuable lessons although she never returns from her descent into the underworld. Charles Smithson travels from the Victorian period into the twentieth century when he encounters the French lieutenant's woman. *Daniel Martin* describes the physical and spiritual wanderings of a contemporary man who also comes to a fuller understanding of himself through the woman he learns to love. In Fowles's next novel the nearly documentary realism of *Daniel Martin* is replaced by fantasy. Although the amnesiac in *Mantissa* never really leaves his hospital room, he sets off on a surrealistic metaphysical odyssey through space and time as he encounters various transformations of the muse who inspires artistic creativity. The embodiment of that muse as a punk rock singer clad in black leather forms diabolic shadows around an awesome figure who offers the ailing writer some painful instruction. But the whimsical, playful tone of *Mantissa,* which appeared in 1982, separates it from the intensity and darkness of Fowles's earlier fiction, where demonic elements prevail. The most intriguing example of this earlier Gothic mode involves a confrontation between a selfish young man and a sorcerer in the novel called *The Magus.*

Although superficially different, John Fowles's *The Magus* and Iris Murdoch's *A Severed Head* when examined more closely show some interesting similarities. Both are novels of education in which the protagonist proves to be in dire need of instruction. In each work important lessons are taught by powerful, mysterious figures who often hold a demonic influence over their pupils. And in both cases the learning process of the protagonist resembles a psychological descent into hell. At Pelham Crescent Martin Lynch-Gibbon goes down into the wine cellar of his subconscious mind, while on the Greek island of *The Magus* Nicholas Urfe explores the underground of his psyche.

Another important parallel lies in the first-person point of view that reflects the self-absorption of the protagonist. Just as Martin Lynch-Gibbon's solipsistic tendencies are established early in Murdoch's novel, Nicholas Urfe's fundamental egotism is emphasized with the first person pronoun included ten times in the novel's opening three sentences all of which also begin with "I."[1] Although both men have studied at Oxford, they each need more education in the area of human relationships. Women especially have been victimized by their insensitive egos.

Just as Martin Lynch-Gibbon locks up women in tidy compartments labeled "mistress" and "wife," so does the younger Nicholas Urfe seem categorical when he veers away from a female intellectual who "was as familiar as a species of bird" (*M*, 26). Nicholas also arrives at a party late so that "the ugly girls . . . would have been disposed of." In order to net the species of bird he prefers, he employs a technique which, according to his statistics, must have been successful, for he brags, "By the time I left Oxford I was a dozen girls away from virginity" (*M*, 21). Nicholas's trick involved being cynical and unpredictable but then "like a conjurer with his white rabbit" he would pull out his solitary heart—his loneliness, which proved to be a "deadly weapon with women" (*M*, 21). Making his encounters with the opposite sex even more magical and illusory, Nicholas would always quickly disappear, for he became "almost as neat at ending liaisons as at starting them" (*M*, 21). As a college student, Nicholas arranged most of his affairs during the term breaks so that he could easily terminate them by "having to go back to school," at which time he would wear the "Chesterfieldian mask" instead of the lonely one. The imagery of a conjurer and his masks anticipates the title character, who will turn the tables and use some of the same deceptive techniques on Nicholas himself—a reversal that can support an allegorical interpretation of the novel. In one sense the magus or sorcerer who will function as Nicholas's didactic demon can be seen as part of Nicholas's own mind: in many ways the magus, whose name is Conchis, can represent the protagonist's own moral consciousness. Just as Nicholas deceived young women, Martin Lynch-Gibbon also enchanted Georgie Hands with various illusions (such as a promised trip to New York) before Honor Klein enchanted him and ultimately taught him to preserve his own honor. In spite of the strange personalities they designate, the names of both Honor and Conchis thus assume decidedly moral overtones.

A crucial difference is that in Fowles's novel the satanic instructor turns out to be an older man while in Murdoch's work a formidable yet captivating older woman takes command. Fowles did at one point consider making the magus character female, but the older man who so powerfully influences Nicholas has at his disposal several female assistants.

Another difference between the two books lies in the fact that more time seems to have elapsed between Nicholas's telling the tale and its actual occurrence. His tone tends to be more detached and analytical than Martin's: Nicholas explains, for instance, that his technique with women during his Oxford period "was calculating, but it was caused less by a true coldness than by my narcissistic belief in the importance of the life-style. I mistook the feeling of relief that dropping a girl always brought for a love of freedom" (M, 21).

Nicholas's attitude alters slightly when he meets an Australian girl named Alison Kelly at a party right below his own apartment in Russell Square. After Alison moves in with him, an intense relationship develops, and interestingly the image of the enclosed room surrounding both Georgie Hands and Miranda Grey is also found in this novel. Because the sister of Alison's old boyfriend lives immediately below Nicholas, for a time Alison hardly ever leaves Nicholas's apartment. The protagonist explains:

> I went and bought food, and we talked and slept and made love and danced and cooked meals at all hours, *sous les toits,* as remote from ordinary time as we were from the dull London world outside the windows. (M, 31)

Just as Martin Lynch-Gibbon and Frederick Clegg had closeted girls in secret rooms, so does Nicholas Urfe collect Alison in a room as well as in an "affaire [which] was like no other [he] had been through" (M, 35).

Loving Nicholas far more than he cares for her, Alison wants their relationship to become more than just an "affaire." In a scene where they finally go out to a restaurant Nicholas meets an old Etonian friend and is embarrassed by Alison's accent and by the "difference" between Alison and several more refined girls sitting nearby. Within five weeks Nicholas seems happy that a new teaching job in a distant land—rather than a new term at Oxford—will provide an easy escape from what has become a stifling situation. While Alison provokes several bitter arguments, Nicholas feels relief that "all this" would soon be over. Alison has even discussed thoughts of suicide, whereas after the final separation Nicholas starts to hum and confesses, "it was not a brave attempt to hide my grief, but a revoltingly unclouded desire to celebrate my release" (*M*, 48). Like Martin Lynch-Gibbon in the early section of *A Severed Head*, Nicholas Urfe in the first part of *The Magus* demonstrates a callous indifference to the women he has emotionally imprisoned. And thus both Murdoch and Fowles set the stage for the entrance of the mysterious figures who will jolt these first-person narrators out of their limited point of view and into a new moral perspective.

But while Martin Lynch-Gibbon had to travel only as far as the sulphurous fog at Liverpool Street Station to meet his Satanic mentor, Nicholas Urfe must sail to a remote Greek island before he can begin his nightmarish tour of a psychological hell, carefully designed for him by a wealthy physician who owns a villa called Bourani on the southern end of the island. In London Nicholas whimsically answers a curious newspaper ad offering a position as an English instructor at the Lord Byron School for Boys on the small Greek island of Phraxos. While job hunting, he expresses a Romantic desire to travel: "I needed a new land, a new race, a new language; and, although I couldn't have put it into words then, I needed a new mystery" (*M*, 19). He feels that Greece would supply him with this mystery, as indeed it does, but in ways that he never imagined. Immediately he is enchanted by the wild beauty of the Greek landscape. But the love of the scenic splendor is soon countered by a "contradictory, almost irritating feeling of impotence and inferiority, as if Greece were a woman so sensually provocative that I must fall physically and desperately in love with her, and at the same time so calmly aristocratic that I should never be able to approach her. . . . None of the books I read explained this sinister-fascinating, this Circe-like quality of Greece" (*M*, 49).

The passage introduces one of the many allusions Fowles employs to add mythic and mystical dimensions to his work. For his modern voyager, Greece itself becomes a sorceress who almost immediately begins to separate him from the everyday world. He writes to Alison, but "already she seemed far away, not in distance, not in time, but in some dimension for which there is no name. Reality perhaps" (*M*, 49). Months pass and gradually correspondence with Alison stops altogether. As the spell of the isolated region continues, "The whole island seemed to feel this exile from contemporary reality" (*M*, 56).

Nicholas usually explores the area by himself since most of the other school masters and boys remain blind to the primitive beauty of the island, which they regard as a "self-imposed penal settlement where one came to work, work, work" (*M*, 51). Growing more lonely, he tries to rekindle his old habit of writing poetry; however, he is devastated by the painful awareness of his inadequacy as a poet: "It was an effort not to cry tears of self-pity. My face set into a stiff-mask, like that of an acroterion. I walked for hours and hours and I was in hell" (*M*, 58). This modern Odysseus, who says he used to turn to poetry as a type of "lifeboat," finds himself emotionally shipwrecked: "Now I was in the sea, and the lifeboat had sunk like lead. . . . For days after I filled myself with nothingness; with something more than the old physical and social loneliness—a metaphysical sense of being marooned. It was something almost intangible, like a cancer or tuberculosis" (*M*, 58). Thus as the first part of the book ends, the voyager seems to be sinking as "the pattern of destiny seemed clear: down and down and down" (*M*, 63).

The French epigraph introducing the second part of the book describes a scene from DeSade in which a victim is being tortured on a table bordered by religious paintings and candles. Suggesting a black mass, the image sets an ominous tone for the long middle section of the three-part novel. Although not as pervasive as the sulphurous fog creating the hellish landscape for Honor Klein's entrance into Murdoch's novel, the "pale smoke" curling up from a rooftop serves as the first indication that the secluded villa at the southern end of the island is no longer deserted. Combing the shoreline after he sees the smoke, Nicholas discovers a beach towel and some poetry books opened to various passages underlined in red. One passage includes T. S. Eliot's lines from "Little Gidding":

> We shall not cease from exploration
> And the end of all our exploration
> Will be to arrive where we started
> And know the place for the first time.

As well as alluding to the novel's three-part structure with the setting changing from London to Greece and back to London again, the passage points to the book's didactic theme and the new knowledge that Nicholas must attain before traveling back to England to rediscover Alison.

But another passage by Pound indicates that the journey Nicholas must first make will involve a descent to the underworld:

> This sound came in the dark
> First must thou go the road to hell
> And to the bower of Ceres' daughter Proserpine,
> Through overhanging dark, to see Tiresias,
> Eyeless that was, a shade, that is in hell
> So full of knowing that the beefy men know less than he,
> Ere thou come to thy road's end.
> Knowledge the shade of a shade,

Yet must thou sail after knowledge
Knowing less than drugged beasts

(Canto XIVII)

This passage not only reinforces the comparison between Nicholas and
Odysseus but also appropriately focuses on one of the central themes of
The Cantos—the descent into Hades from Homer. Indeed it soon becomes clear that Nicholas Urfe, like Martin Lynch-Gibbon, must plunge
to the deepest regions of his soul before he can bloom into a more
sensitive moral being. And while Murdoch's protagonist is led to the
lower depths by Honor Klein, Nicholas Urfe is conducted on a tour
through hell by the wealthy owner of the remote villa, an exotic individual named Maurice Conchis.

Malcolm Bradbury has compared Conchis to "the psychopomp figures
of Iris Murdoch's early novels—Hugo Belfounder, Mischa Fox, Honor
Klein—with their ambiguous philosophical or anthropological charisma
. . . [who represent] forces beyond and outside the familiar orders of
society and its states of mind, possessors of ambiguous myths that yet
contain both truth and falsehood."[2] Bradbury maintains that Conchis's
suprarational knowledge "has the prophetic pull of Honor Klein's dark
wisdom in *A Severed Head,* and the same sense that it is a knowledge
beyond the novel's capacity to register. . . . [As] with *A Severed Head,* the
rationalistic underpinning of day-to-day life, with its casual sexual relationships and its vague code of personal relations, is left behind."[3]

One might extend Bradbury's analysis to certain polarities in the
novels of Muriel Spark, such as the tension between the normally com-
placent village of Peckham Rye and Douglas Dougal, the curious outsider with bumps on his head. All three authors use demonic imagery to
emphasize the dark powers of their exotic, charismatic figures. And in
tracing a line from Honor Klein to Douglas Dougal to Maurice Conchis,
one does begin to notice a gathering of devils in contemporary British
fiction. Their creators undoubtedly feel that powerful compelling forces
are needed to blast society out of its moral lethargy.

When Nicholas finally meets Conchis, for instance, his first impression
resembles that of Martin Lynch-Gibbon confronting the formidable
Honor Klein:

> The most striking thing about him was the intensity of his eyes; very
> dark brown, staring with a simian penetration emphasized by the
> remarkably clear whites; eyes that seemed not quite human. . . .
> There was something mask-like, emotion-purged, about his face.
> Deep furrows ran from beside his nose to the corners of his mouth;
> they suggested experience, command, impatience with fools. He was
> slightly mad. . . . He kept his ape-like eyes on me. The silence and the

stare were alarming . . . as if he was trying to hypnotize a bird. (*M*, 79–80)

Several images in this passage continue to ripple throughout the novel. The element of disguise prevails. After one of many strange occurrences on the island Nicholas looks to Conchis for an answer only to confront the "blank mask of his face" (*M*, 185). Similarly a number of Conchis's associates wear both literal and figurative masks (*M*, 196, 204, 205). The hypnosis imagery also continues. Enigmatic and mysterious, Conchis does actually hypnotize Nicholas after dinner one evening but countless other times captivates Nicholas with his "naturally mesmeric eyes" (*M*, 237).

Although Nicholas's curiosity is aroused by Conchis's appearance, the protagonist finds his host's actions even more inscrutable. Besides making cryptic comments, Conchis produces for Nicholas a series of psychodramas or bizarre tableaus that he collectively refers to as "The Masque." Various figures in the masque soon walk offstage and into Nicholas's life so that the young man finds it increasingly difficult to distinguish between illusion and reality. In time he suspects that Conchis is manipulating him for some unknown reason by using these talented performers who never really remove their masks either on or off the stage. Indeed the whole concept of stage and audience disapppears as the protagonist becomes more involved in the series of dramas. But the deception becomes so pervasive, that Nicholas learns to distrust Conchis and frequently refers to him as that same Arch-trickster who taunted the citizens of Peckham Rye. Whenever Nicholas feels that perhaps Conchis has shut down his strange theater, he is made to realize that the apparent end proves to be only an intermission: "The masque had moved outside the domaine, and the old devil had not given in one bit" (*M*, 373).

The Satanic references become even more appropriate when in one strange episode Nicholas finds himself imprisoned in an underground chamber and facing the devil himself:

> The head was that of a pure black goat: a real goat's head, worn as a kind of cap, so that it stood high off the shoulders of the person beneath, whose real face must have lain behind the shaggy beard. Huge backswept horns, left their natural colour; amber glass eyes; the only ornament, a fat blood-red candle that had been fixed between the horns and lit. . . . I realized that he was lampooning the traditional Christ-figure; the staff was the pastoral crook, the black beard Christ's brown one, the blood-red candle some sort of blasphemous parody of the halo. . . . The goat figure, his satanic majesty, came forward with an archdiabolical dignity and I braced myself for the next development: a black Mass seemed likely. (*M*, 502)

After being tied to a whipping post and psychologically tormented, Nicholas considers himself to be "chained in hell" (*M*, 530). Thus one need not search far to find demonic imagery—all of which reinforces the point that the protagonist not only is spending an unusual year on a Greek island but also is embarking upon a journey through Hades. As Nicholas says, "Always with Conchis one went down, and it seemed one could go no farther; but at the end another way went even lower" (*M*, 515).

But like Honor Klein, the demonic Maurice Conchis also proves to be didactic. For the strange masque is designed to show Nicholas that the real devil is lodged within his own soul—especially in his callous treatment of young women like Alison. Many of the tableaus performed on that Greek island reflect Nicholas's own selfish nature. But only gradually does this first-person narrator begin to understand Conchis's cryptic remark: "Greece is like a mirror. It makes you suffer. Then you learn" (*M*, 99).

Conchis's didactic technique also involves a series of narrations about his own past, parts of which often serve as the central themes of the psychodramas performed by his troupe of players. Nicholas gradually learns that even more parallels exist between the masque and his own life. Layer upon layer, Chinese box within Chinese box, world within world—the protagonist becomes increasingly confused as illusion merges with reality. After one peculiar episode where a seventeenth-century murderer is resurrected in a tableau in the forest, Nicholas says:

> I stood there in the trees, absolutely at a loss . . . I had somehow landed myself in the centre of an extraordinary old man's fantasies. That was clear. Why he should hold them, why he should so strangely realize them, and above all, why he should have chosen me to be his solitary audience of one, remained a total mystery. But I knew I had become involved in something too uniquely bizarre to miss. (*M*, 143)

In spite of his enchantment, Nicholas begins to feel more and more like a victim, a "fly" at the mercy of Conchis who is perpetually "weaving his web" (*M*, 127). As the masque continues, the protagonist also realizes that his role has changed from observer to participant.

After an especially frustrating encounter with one of the actresses, Nicholas finds himself deserted near an old cistern in the forest. Soon, however, he has company:

> A brilliant red-and-black jumping spider edged along the puteal towards me. I laid my hand in its path and it jumped on it; holding it up close I could see its minute black eyes, like gig-lamps. It swivelled its massive square head from side to side in an arachnoidal parody of

> Conchis's quizzing; and once again . . . I had an uncanny apprehen-
> sion of a reality of witchcraft; Conchis's haunting, brooding omnipre-
> sence. (*M*, 386)

And when one of the players pretends to remove her mask and read
Nicholas a psychological report about the entire Bourani "experiment,"
Nicholas says:

> I stared at her, but she would not look up. I knew who had written the
> report. There were too many echoes of Conchis. I was not misled by
> the new mask. He was still the master of ceremonies, the man behind it
> all; at web center. (*M*, 511)

The spider motif especially emphasizes the protagonist's feeling of being
trapped.

Fowles also relies upon imagery involving skulls and skeletons to etch
in the novel's demonic shading. Conchis informs Nicholas that the name
Bourani is derived from a Greek word that means both gourd and skull,
suggesting both water and death. The more negative connotation is
reinforced by numerous scenes throughout the book. In the forest, for
example, a grim lesson seems intended when Nicholas confronts a
death's-head hanging from a tree. A recalcitrant student, he actually toys
with this macabre figure:

> I twisted the skull and made it spin. Shadows haunted the sockets, the
> mouth grinned grimly. (*M*, 460)

Nicholas's game with death parallels the way he has played with other
people's lives. In another scene even though Nicholas at first senses that
the inside of Conchis's mansion "was as quiet as death, as the inside of a
skull," he reassures himself that "the year was 1953. I was an atheist and
an absolute non-believer in spiritualism, ghosts and all that mumbo-
jumbo" (*M*, 102). Yet in spite of his protests, the protagonist perceives
ominous shadows surrounding the owner of the villa:

> Conchis grimaced. . . . His skin clung very close to his skull. Only the
> eyes lived. I had the strange impression that he wanted me to believe
> he was death; that at any moment the leathery old skin and the eyes
> would fall, and I should find myself the guest of a skeleton. (*M*, 99)

One of the most important motifs contributing to the novel's mysterious
atmosphere is introduced by the book's title. As a result of his diabolic
trickery Conchis is associated with the Magus of the Tarot cards and in
one phantasmagoric tableau even appears as such with a tall peaked hat,
black mask and gloves, and a cloak with astrological symbols. Later

Nicholas is walking by an antique shop and notices five old Tarot cards propped up in the window: "On one of them was a man dressed exactly as Conchis had been; even to the same emblems on his cloak. Underneath were the words *LE SORCIER*—the sorcerer" (*M*, 579).

In *The Key to the Tarot* Arthur Edward Waite describes the first card of the Tarot deck as "The Magus, Magician, or Juggler, the caster of dice and mountebank in the world of vulgar trickery. This is the colportage interpretation, and it has the same correspondence with the real symbolic meaning that the use of the Tarot in fortune telling has with its mystic construction according to the secret science of symbolism."[4] Like Waite, most authorities on the Tarot disparage the use of the cards as mere fortune-telling devices and instead look to them for mystical truths about the human soul and the cosmos. In *A New Model of the Universe* P. D. Ouspensky writes: "the pack of Tarot cards, according to legend, represents an Egyptian hieroglyphic book, consisting of seventy-eight tablets, which have come down to us in a miraculous manner. . . . Outwardly the Tarot is a pack of cards, but in its inner meaning it is something altogether different. It is a 'book' of philosophical and psychological content, which can be read in many ways."[5]

Parallels to the Tarot cards ripple through *The Magus*. The Tarot deck consists of seventy-eight cards; the novel contains seventy-eight chapters. Two of Conchis's assistants are the twin sisters, Lily and Rose, who are named after two symbols found on the Magus's card, the lily suggesting purity and the rose, passion. At first Lily Montgomery plays an innocent role while her sister Rose pretends to be more aggressive and flirtatious. But when Alison reenters the plot, Lily assumes a more seductive role. In many ways Nicholas parallels the card called the Fool, which depicts a young man strolling along, unaware that he walks dangerously close to a precipice. Nicholas does, of course, plunge headlong into the bizarre world of Bourani as he suggests in one of his poems:

From this skull-rock strange golden roots throw
  Ikons and incidents: the man in the mask
Manipulates. I am the fool that falls
And never learns to wait and watch,
  Icarus eternally damned, the dupe of time.

(M, 95)

Later he tries to transcend this role when he says about Conchis, "I'll seem his fool, but not be his fool" (*M*, 137).

Critics have hunted for even more intricate correspondences,[6] but more important than all the one-to-one parallels, the system of reading the Tarot cards in many ways reflects the symbolic technique of the novel. In his book on hermetic symbolism Oswald Wirth has written:

A symbol can always be studied from an infinite number of points of view; and each thinker has the right to discover in the symbol a new meaning corresponding to the logic of his own conceptions. As a matter of fact symbols are precisely intended to awaken ideas sleeping in our consciousness. They arouse a thought by means of suggestion and thus cause the truth which lies hidden in the depths of our spirit to reveal itself.[7]

Discussing the symbolism of the Tarot cards, P. D. Ouspensky adds that symbols "cannot speak to everyone. They especially elude minds which claim to be positive and which base their reasoning only on inert scientific and dogmatic formulae."[8] Thus Lily rebukes Nicholas when he insists on playing detective and finding all the trapdoors rather than surrendering himself to the imaginative truth of the tableaus. At one point she asks him, "Why must you always know where you are?" (*M*, 197). Ouspensky concludes, "By their very nature symbols must remain elastic, vague and ambiguous, like the sayings of an oracle. Their role is to unveil mysteries, leaving the mind all its freedom."[9]

Throughout the novel Nicholas struggles with the oblique, symbolic technique of the magus. When locked in an underground cell, Nicholas rants: "I . . . seethed trying to comprehend the sadistic old man's duplicities: to read his palimpsest. . . . Perhaps what he was doing did spring in part from some theory of the theatre, but he had said it himself: The masque is only a metaphor. So? Some incomprehensible new philosophy: metaphorism? Perhaps he saw himself as a professor in an impossible faculty of ambiguity, a sort of Empson of the event. I thought and thought, and thought again, and arrived at last at nothing but more doubt" (*M*, 458).

Frequently a tale about Conchis's past life will be reflected in one of the psychodramas which in turn will also mirror some element in Nicholas's life. This method again echoes the technique of the Tarot pack composed, as one scholar says, "of numbers and figures, which mutually react upon and explain each other."[10] Thus, beyond any itemized correspondence, the shifting symbolic method of reading the Tarot cards parallels the shifting symbolic method of *The Magus*.

Old devils, Satanic goats, enchanted spiders, death-skulls, Tarot cards, and sorcerers—all help to create the demonic atmosphere of the novel. Reinforced by the many underground cells and tunnels, the pervasive metaphor of the labyrinth also contributes to the sense of esoteric mystery. Fowles has indicated that he once considered calling his book *The Maze*. And Nicholas often uses the metaphor to describe his confusion. Just before a nocturnal rendezvous with Lily he comments, "My heart was beating faster than it should. It was partly at the thought of meeting her, partly at something far more mysterious, the sense that I was now deep in the strangest maze in Europe. Now I really was Theseus; somewhere in the darkness Ariadne waited; and perhaps the Minotaur" (*M*, 313). Several of Conchis's disciples tell Nicholas that they too are working their way through the labyrinth of Conchis's psychological experiments, but later these "revelations" also prove to be only more false turns. After apologizing to Nicholas for "all the peculiar mazes through which [they] have made [him] run" (*M*, 507), the alleged psychologists themselves dissolve into mere illusions in the ingeniously deceptive labyrinth designed by that arch-trickster, the Magus. Even after he leaves the island and questions Mitford, the former English instructor at the boys' school, Nicholas remains uncertain about how far he can trust his predecessor, who he believes has also experienced The Masque: "Again I surreptitiously eyed him; knew myself lost in the interminable maze of echoes. Was he, or wasn't he?" (*M*, 615).

In a photographic essay called *Islands* Fowles writes about some actual stone mazes he found on the treacherous Scilly Islands off Cornwall, England. He then discusses the archetypal significance of both mazes and islands for several works of literature, especially *The Odyssey*, which he says strongly influenced *The Magus*. After analyzing Odysseus's various encounters with Circe and Calypso, Fowles comments: "The sea and its islands thus become the domain of what cannot be controlled by wisdom and reason; the laboratory where the guinea pig Odysseus must run through the mazes; where the great ally of reason, the conscious, gives way to the rule of the unconscious and the libido, that eternal and oceanic unsettler of domestic peace and established order."[11] Even after Odysseus returns to Ithaca, he still has not reached the center of the maze because, as Fowles sees it, "there is a famous thread left lying loose at the end,"[12] the fact that Odysseus knows from Tiresias that he must make still another voyage until he reaches the people who know nothing of the sea. Thus for Odysseus, and perhaps for Nicholas too, Fowles maintains, "The sea, the invitation to the unknown, will remain the unassuaged demon."[13]

This demon will repeatedly force the voyager to come to the island of his own being. Fowles writes, "No recurrent symbolism in *The Odyssey* is more pertinent than the long and deliberate stripping its hero undergoes: of his ships, of his men, of his hopes, of his clothes, even of his very skin on the cliffs of Corfu."[14] Similarly in *The Magus* Nicholas loses his "lifeboat" of poetic inspiration, appears naked in several scenes including the episode where he is drugged and abducted, and in a reenactment of a World War II incident scrapes the skin off his hand.

Exploring the maze imagery in another island story that influenced *The Magus*, Fowles could easily be describing his own technique when he says of *The Tempest:* "Shakespeare made his over-riding metaphors the

island and the sailor stranded in a place that he cannot fully understand
. . . that both bewitches and is intensely cruel, that can hold both Cal-
ibans and Ariels, Antonios and Mirandas, that can be only too savagely
'real' and yet still an insubstantial pageant."[15] Frequently alluding to
Shakespeare's play, Nicholas often sees himself as Ferdinand to Conchis's
Prospero (*M*, 136, 204, 341), but after being taunted so much with the
Lily-Julie figure, the protagonist concludes: "But this was Prospero
turned insane, maniacally determined never to release his Miranda" (*M*,
458).

In additional commentary on the history of the labyrinth Fowles writes
that "in both Celtic and Mediterranean Europe the maze appears to be
associated with the tomb; and escape from it with reincarnation."[16] He
believes this interpretation lies at the heart of the Daedalus legend of
Minoan Crete, where a maze pattern was used in ancient spring fertility
dances. Certainly in *The Magus* all the tunnel and skull imagery reinforces the idea of a tomb. One of the novel's most crucial scenes occurs in
a large underground room actually called "Earth," and Fowles has indicated that Nicholas Urfe's last name was derived from the author's
childhood inability to pronounce the same term.[17] As he descends into
his hellish tomb, Nicholas Urfe therefore goes further and further into
himself. The author's essay also explains that the center of the maze "lies
not in the unravelled, but the unravelling."[18] For various older cultures
and certainly for Nicholas too "maze-center represented true self-knowl-
edge."[19]

Thus Fowles ultimately finds great value in islands because "of their
nature they question . . . properly experienced, they make us stop and
think a little: why am I here, what am I about, what is it all about, what
has gone wrong? . . . Islands strip and dissolve the crud of our cultural
accretions, the Odyssean mask of victim we all wear: I am this because
life has made me like this, not because I really want to be like this."[20]
Such a mask is worn by Nicholas in the early part of the novel when he
says on the first page, "I lacked the parents and ancestors I needed,"
when he frequently relies upon the passive voice ("I was born . . . I was
sent to a public school"), and when he later sinks into depression and
blames the world for his inability to write poetry. It will take a hellish
experience to make Nicholas strip off the crud of his cultural accretions,
come to the island of his own being, take responsibility for his actions,
and ask in an existential sense, "Who am I?"

A hellish experience is exactly what the demonic Conchis has con-
cocted for Nicholas Urfe. Fowles undoubtedly sees advantages in the
painful journey Nicholas must make, for in one sense he himself has just
completed a similar excursion in writing *The Magus*. He comments in
Islands: "The real Ulysses is whoever wrote the *Odyssey*, is Joyce, is every

artist who sets off into the unknown of his own unconscious and knows he must run the gauntlet of the island reefs, the monsters, the sirens, the Calypsos and the Circes, with only a very dim faith that an Athene [or a Mantissa?] is somewhere there to help and a wise Penelope waiting at the end."[21]

But if both Fowles and his protagonist must travel through the treacherous labyrinth, the reader must certainly follow. The masks, the changing personalities, the various mythical and literary identities, and the abrupt turns in the plot—all reinforce the metaphor of the maze from the structural point of view. Characters switch identities as fast as Theseus turned corners in the labyrinth so that the reader also is forced to become both an adventurer and a guinea pig who must work his way through the snares designed by the ultimate magus, sorcerer, and didactic demon—John Fowles himself.

The very act of reading the novel becomes a type of odyssey through a strange illusory realm frequently resembling hell. Critics often describe "the many plot convolutions through which the author . . . lures his readers."[22] To add credibility, Fowles makes his narrator skeptical. For example, Nicholas refers to one of the mythological tableaus featuring unclothed performers as "last night's strip show" (M, 196). The protagonist even occasionally tries to create his own subterfuge; he writes about a conversation with Lily: "I left a little silence, as a test, knowing that liars hate silence. But she passed that" (M, 342). Disarmed by Nicholas's cautious skepticism, the reader is carried along by the author's craftmanship, especially his strong narrative line and his ingenious use of suspense. The reader therefore tends to believe Nicholas when he feels he has at last uncovered the reality behind the illusion, but all too frequently both protagonist and reader are duped when even the "final" veil reveals yet another veil underneath. At one point Lily speaks fairly truthfully when she talks about the "place of mystery in life. Not taking anything for granted. A world where nothing is certain. That's what [Conchis] is trying to create here" (M, 339). James Lindroth has described the novel as a "love-mystery story in which relationships and identities continually shift."[23] As a result of all the mirror images, puzzles, psychological chess games, and hallucinatory demonic imagery, the reader often feels as if he is wandering through some surrealistic labyrinth. This sensation perhaps explains why in the 1960s and '70s *The Magus* became a cult object among many college students, who—speaking more truth than they knew—asked Fowles what type of "trip" he was on when he wrote the novel.

Also supporting the book's labyrinthian structure, the network of literary and mythic references contributes to the novel's complexity as it reinforces the archetypal dimensions of the protagonist. As Nicholas

recognizes while walking back to school after another mysterious interlude at Bourani, "The events of the week-end seemed to recede, to
become locked away, as if I had dreamt them; and yet as I walked there
came the strangest feeling, compounded of the early hour, the absolute
solitude, and what had happened, of having entered a myth; a knowledge of what it was like physically, moment by moment, to have been
young and ancient, a Ulysses on his way to meet Circe, a Theseus on his
journey to Crete, an Oedipus still searching for his destiny" (*M*, 157).

If Nicholas is cast as Ulysses from the Homeric myth, Lily is undoubtedly assigned "the Circe role" (*M*, 564). Lily serves as the lure Conchis
uses in his continual enchantment of Nicholas Urfe. As the protagonist
tries to explain to Alison after a brief idyllic excursion to Mount Parnassus, he must return to Phraxos because "I only know I'm haunted,
possessed" (*M*, 275). And although he thinks he is jesting, he later speaks
accurately when he says that he has "given his soul to a witch" (*M*, 344).
Recalling his insensitivity toward Alison, he also explains, "I was like one
of Ulysses's sailors—turned into a swine" (*M*, 279).

As she beguiles Nicholas, this modern sorceress undergoes a series of
transformations: Lily Montgomery, the genteel ghost of Conchis's dead
Edwardian fiancée; Julie Holmes, an actress originally hired to make an
unusual movie on the Greek island; a schizophrenic, whose mad tan-
trums must be carefully managed; Dr. Vanessa Maxwell, an eminent
psychologist who has been studying Nicholas's behavior in a scientific
experiment. Sometimes Nicholas perceives more than one personality at
a time. While Conchis, Nicholas, and Lily are watching an obscene
tableau from the patio, Nicholas, for instance, notices that the Lily
Montgomery mask begins to slip: "I slid a quick look at the girl beside
me. I thought I detected a faint smile, a kind of excitement at cruelty,
even when being mimed, that I did not like: it was very remote from the
Edwardian 'other' world whose clothes she still wore" (*M*, 182). The face
behind all these faces, however, belongs to a demon lover who mes-
merizes Nicholas with her unearthly beauty. She entices Nicholas down
one pathway of the maze after another. Even though she often deceives
him, he frequently rationalizes her actions: "I was shown a new vista: the
possibility that she had been playing her part under some form of
duress" (*M*, 209). But all "vistas" turn into mere illusions as Conchis and
his lovely assistant continue to refine their diabolic craft.

After an erotic swim in the ocean with this Circe figure, Nicholas
begins to describe the influence of both the temptress and her twin
sister:

Julie entranced me. It was as if I had stumbled on a sleeping princess
and found her, once woken, not merely in love with me, but erotically

starved, deliciously eager to exorcize whatever sour and perverse lovemaking had gone on with her ill-starved choice of the previous year. I imagined a Julie who had acquired all Alison's experience and adeptness, her quick passions, her slow lubricities, but enhanced, enriched, diversified by superior taste, intelligence, poetry . . . I kept smiling to myself as I walked. There was a thin new moon, the starlight, and I now knew almost by heart my way up through the ghostly, silent forest of Aleppo pines. I saw nothing in the present, only the endless seduction and surrender of that willing body: nights in the village house, indolent naked siestas on some shadowed bed . . . and when we were satiated, that other, golden lapping presence, June, implicit two for the price of one. Of course it was Julie I loved, but all love needs a teasing, a testing dry relief. (*M*, 371)

The passage demonstrates the way in which Julie leads Nicholas into the realm of fantasy and illusion. The "sleeping princess," the "thin new moon," the "ghostly silent forest," and the "golden lapping presence"—all belong to the dreamy language of enchantment. The two ellipses, the long flowing sentences, and the fuzziness of perception in phrases such as "some shadowed bed" suggest a mind drifting off into an illusory world. The formation of an ideal lover with traits of both Alison and Julie recalls Miranda's imaginary composite man in *The Collector*. And like Martin Lynch-Gibbon, Nicholas begins to stage a solipsistic drama peopled not with one but two phantom lovers—Julie and her twin sister June, who would be present simply to provide a "teasing" and "testing dry relief." For a while Nicholas keeps smiling to himself.

But this happy reverie forms only half of a pattern that keeps repeating itself. Again and again Conchis turns Nicholas's blissful daydreams into raging nightmares. In another scene Nicholas feels that Julie has finally come over to his side because she reveals an underground tunnel that Conchis has used in various "supernatural" scenes in the forest. But as Julie climbs the ladder out of the underground cell:

Someone, perhaps two someones, had sprung from behind the lid and grabbed her arms. She seemed to be lifted, almost jerked bodily out and away—a leg kicked wildly sideways, as if she were trying to hook a foot behind the counterweight wires. My name again, but cut short; a scuffle of stones outside, out of my sight. I clawed violently up the remaining rungs. For one fraction of a second a face appeared in the opening above. A young man with crewcut blond hair, the sailor I had seen that morning at the house. He saw I was still two rungs from the top, and immediately slammed the lid down. The shocked counterweights rattled against the metal wall by my feet. I bellowed in the sudden darkness. (*M*, 458)

Here the fragmented style contrasts sharply to the mellifluous tone of the previous passage. The dash, the short choppy sentences, the staccato effect—all parallel the painful interruption of Nicholas's pleasant fantasies as the hollering protagonist finds himself once again dropped into hell. Thus Nicholas is made to see that harsh reality will inevitably intrude into an illusory world. The body-snatching, of course, represents another theatrical trick in Conchis's drama, yet, as one of the actresses later tells Nicholas, in many ways the masque approaches psychological truth more closely than does reality itself. The ultimately didactic episode mirrors the various disappearing acts that Nicholas himself has performed before a series of enchanted females who had been assigned only temporary roles in the young man's fantasies.

Even in the early tableaus, grotesque and obscene as some of them are, a didactic undercurrent can be detected. One evening, for instance, as Conchis, Lily, and Nicholas are relaxing on the patio after dinner, a loud horn disturbs the evening. Nicholas is simply told that it is Apollo. Soon Nicholas sees in the nearby forest a large naked man illuminated by a spotlight. Wearing a wreath on his head, the Apollo figure presides over the strange scene that unfolds. A beautifully supple nymph, also unclothed, is pursued by a swarthy satyr with a grotesquely enlarged phallus rising from his loins. Soon another person representing Artemis appears on the scene equipped with a silver bow and arrow: "Something in her stance, as well as the distorted face, was genuinely frightening" (*M*, 182). Before long Artemis stalks the satyr and shoots him in the heart with the swift arrow. As Nicholas is trying to interpret the bizarre tableau, he thinks:

> I felt unsure, out of my depth, a lot more innocent and unsophisticated at heart than I liked to pretend. . . . More and more I smelt some nasty drift in Conchis's divertimenti. That phallus, the nakedness, the naked girl. . . . I had an idea that sooner or later I was going to be asked to perform as well, that this was some initiation to a much darker adventure that I was prepared for, a society, a cult. (*M*, 182, 184)

Nicholas is right. Conchis will try to show him that he is already cast in the plot, playing the role of the satyr as indeed he has spent his lust on a variety of young girls. Conchis will provide his own special nymphs to lure Nicholas through a psychological forest, but the ardent young man will pursue these dream figures as relentlessly as did the satyr, only to be thwarted again and again. That a moral lesson is intended in the tableau can be seen by the intervention of Artemis who herself becomes a type of didactic demon with her "eyes elongated by black make-up, and the hair . . . also elongated backwards in a way that was classical yet sinister" (*M*, 182). As Fowles notes in his article called "The Trouble With Starlets," which analyzes nymphs and goddesses of the twentieth century: "Man's adoration of woman has taken many forms . . . Artemis (Diana), goddess of the moon, of chastity, of lust controlled, reaches far back into civilization, and she was perhaps the earliest of all man's attempts to turn himself into a moral being."[24] This particular interpretation of Artemis is undoubtedly the one Conchis intended, but only gradually does Nicholas realize the significance of her role as well as that of the swarthy satyr, a mythological creature which Conchis uses to show Nicholas that the real darkness, as Conrad suggested, lies within one's own heart.

Along with mythological tableaus, narrations about Conchis's own life begin to weave a web of obscure meaning around Nicholas's confused mind. Conchis's first stories include accounts from his more unsophisticated earlier years. An intense chapter from this period involves an obsessed backwoodsman who becomes for the aspiring physician a type of fiendish instructor. The imagery in this episode accentuates the polarity between an ordered, scientific realm and a more violent, irrational world, as an ornithological expedition brings the curious young biology student to a remote northern section of Norway known as the Seidvarre. Here Conchis temporarily resides with Gustav Nygaard, an educated farmer; the farmer's sister-in-law; and her two children. Also a bird enthusiast, Gustav seems evasive when the young naturalist asks him about his absent brother. Since Conchis had been "conditioned by a kind of ornithological approach to man" (M, 308), he soon tracks down the "missing" brother, who lives as a hermit in a primitive cabin on a peninsula about half a mile from the farm. Gustav finally explains that for the last twelve years his nearly blind brother Henrik has alienated himself from the rest of mankind as he waits insanely on his isolated peninsula for a meeting with the Holy Spirit in the form of a pillar of fire. Intrigued by "this rare specimen of humanity" (M, 304), Conchis begins to "stalk and watch Henrik like a bird" (M, 303). Focusing his field glasses from a safe distance like the governess in *The Unicorn*, the young naturalist observes that Henrik appears to be a tall

> thin man with rough-cut dark-grey hair and beard and an aquiline nose. He turned by chance and faced us and I had a full view of his gaunt face. What surprised me was its fierceness. A severity that was almost savagery. I had never seen a face that expressed such violent determination never to compromise, never to deviate. Never to smile. And what eyes! They were slightly exopthalmic, of the most startling cold blue. Beyond any doubt, insane eyes. Even at fifty yards I could see that. (M, 304)

What the naive student cannot immediately see in this demonic portrait, however, is the reason behind the obsession of its subject. But just as Iris Murdoch's characters in *A Severed Head* tried to build a framework of

gentility over a stream of turbulent passions, just as Frederick Clegg
wanted to pin down his fluttering captive, just as Nicholas himself
attempted to classify a "familiar . . . species of bird" (*M*, 26) during the
party at Russell Square, so does the young ornithologist attempt to throw
a net of civilized theories over this "fierce blinded hawk of a man" (*M*,
304). As the older Conchis admits, "Up to this point in my life you will
have realized that my whole approach was scientific, medical, classify-
ing. . . . I thought in terms of species, behavior, observations" (*M*, 308).
But when the young scientist actually approaches the crude cabin and
tries to reason with Henrik about "modern methods of treatment for
cataract," Henrik's response recalls that of Honor Klein who slashed
through the civilized structure that Antonia and Palmer Anderson
erected around Martin Lynch-Gibbon. While Honor Klein resorted to a
Samurai sword, Henrik Nygaard uses an ax. A truly Satanic figure,
Henrik swings his sharp weapon at the logical brain of his young visitor
and misses him only because of his poor eyesight. Henrik then plunges
the deadly ax into a silver birch, "a fair sized tree. But it shook from top
to bottom with the blow. And that was his answer" (*M*, 306).

Although he casts demonic shadows, Henrik Nygaard also proves to
be instructive. An older Conchis recounts the fiery lesson he learned that
day at the Seidvarre as he acknowledges, "I went back to the farmstead a
wiser young man" (*M*, 306). Again in a way that recalls *A Severed Head*,
Conchis explains, "That axe would have driven right through the skull of
all our pleasure-orientated civilization. Our science, our psycho-analysis.
To him all that was what the Buddhists call lilas—the futile pursuit of
triviality. And of course to have been concerned about his blindness
would have been for him more futility. He wanted to be blind. It made it
more likely that one day he would see" (*M*, 306).

Later that evening Conchis observes Henrik crying out to his lord as
he kneels in a foot of water out on the peninsula. All of the young man's
scientific theories are shattered when he suddenly realizes that Henrik is
no longer waiting to meet his God but is actually confronting Him out on
the water. The violent imagery continues but with didactic overtones as
Conchis concludes:

> in a flash, as of lightning, all our explanations, all our classifications
> and derivations, our aetiologies, suddenly appeared to me like a thin
> net. That great passive monster, reality, was no longer dead, easy to
> handle. It was full of a mysterious vigour, new forms, new possibilities.
> The net was nothing, reality burst through it. (*M*, 309)

At the end of the Seidvarre story Conchis dovetails the account with
another episode from his past that he had related much earlier in the

novel. The two stories counterpoint each other in that they focus on two diametrically opposed personalities, the first narration involving a wealthy aristocrat who befriended Conchis when he overheard the young man playing the harpsichord. While Henrik's story took place in the northern wilderness, the story of Alphonse de Deukans began in the cultural center of Paris and moved to the beautiful French countryside. Henrik occupied a foul smelling cabin decorated only by two biblical quotations etched in blood; de Deukans resided in a great chateau in eastern France known as Givray-le-Duc. Henrik wore rags; de Deukans was "faultlessly dressed, a gardenia in his buttonhole" (*M*, 175). While Henrik owned no material objects save a Bible and an ax, de Deukans provided the ultimate example of what Fowles has called the "collector consciousness." Alphonse de Deukans presided over a great palace:

> which was nothing more nor less than a vast museum. There were countless galleries, of paintings, of porcelains, of *objets d'art* of all kinds. . . . An armoury. A cabinet of Greek and Roman coins. I could inventory all night, for he had devoted all his life to this collecting of collections. (*M*, 177)

While Henrik looked for heaven in another world, de Deukans tried to emulate heaven in this world. The luxuriant grounds on his estate were arranged to provide various ambiences and decors: a classical temple; a rotunda; English, Oriental, and Moorish gardens.

But as in the case of Frederick Clegg, certain items in de Deukans's collections created a hellish rather than heavenly ambience. Encased in a medieval reliquary in his private chapel lay an object resembling a withered sea-cucumber that de Deukans called the Holy Member. This blasphemous object had no special significance for the Frenchman. As Conchis explained, "This is true of all collecting. It extinguishes the moral instinct. The object finally possesses the possessor" (*M*, 178). This last statement gains a literal significance in the form of one particularly hellish item in de Deukans's bizarre collection of automata or life-sized puppets. Featured in this collection was a startling device created for the Sultan of Turkey and called:

> Mirabelle, la Maitresse-Machine. A naked woman, painted and silk-skinned, who when set in motion lay back in her faded four-poster bed, drew up her knees and then opened them together with her arms. As her human master lay on top of her, the arms closed and held him. But de Deukans cherished her most because she had a device that made it unlikely that she would ever cuckold her owner. Unless one moved a small lever at the back of her head, at a certain pressure her arms would clasp with vice-like strength. And then a

stiletto on a strong spring struck upwards through the adulterer's groin. (*M,* 177–78)

Besides demonstrating the perversity that a mechanized civilization can cultivate, Mirabelle gives an ironic twist to the notion of demonic didacticism. An appropriate symbol of Givray-le-Duc, the deadly Mirabelle reigned as its true mistress because de Deukans, a radical misogynist, allowed no real woman to enter his sprawling chateau: "All his servants were like himself—silent, grave-looking men" (*M,* 176).

Although polite and refined, the aristocrat made the perfect partner for the grotesque Mirabelle—especially in his cold, mechanical indifference to the suffering of others. He lacked any sense of social responsibility. When Conchis and he passed some peasants struggling in a turnip field, de Deukans, like Effingham Cooper, turned the situation into an aesthetic experience, remarking, "It is beautiful that they are they and that we are we" (*M,* 178). Thus while Henrik Nygaard suffered from actual blindness, Alphonse de Deukans remained blind to the misfortune of his fellow men. Conchis even compares de Deukans to the evil Kurtz in Joseph Conrad's novel. Discussing the French aristocrat's wealth, Conchis explains, "He had large estates in Belgium. Investments in France and Germany. But the great bulk of his money was in various enterprises in the Congo. Givray-le-Duc, like the Parthenon, was built on a heart of darkness" (*M,* 188). Yet in spite of the grim implication in his statement, Conchis was enchanted by the order and harmony of Givray-le-Duc with its lush gardens and intriguing collections. The medical student sometimes considered de Deukans as a "man from a perfect world lost in a very imperfect one" (*M,* 180). And just as he realized the implacable determination in Henrik Nygaard, he also found de Deukans "determined with a monomania . . . to maintain his perfections" (*M,* 180). But one day the perfect peace and order of Givray-le-Duc were interrupted by a woman's laughter. This intrusive sound was made by a girlfriend of one of the younger servants, who had smuggled her into the palace and as a result of his bold venture was soon fired. Teaching his former master a diabolic lesson, the servant later retaliated by burning down the grand chateau, which now even more clearly resembled hell rather than heaven:

> Every painting was shrivelled, every book ashes, every piece of porcelain twisted and smoked, every coin melted, every piece of furniture, each automaton, even Mirabelle, charred to nothingness. All that was left were parts of the walls and the eternally irreparable. (*M,* 187)

Two days afterward in his Paris apartment de Deukans killed himself with an overdose of drugs. His valet reported that he found his master "with a kind of sneer on his face. It had shocked the man" (*M*, 187). The sneer recalls Kurtz's comment—"The horror. The horror"—when he too looked straight into the abyss that mocks the ambition behind all men's collections.

After Conchis tells the story of Henrik Nygaard, he remarks: "I saw Henrik meet his pillar of fire at about midnight on August 17, 1922. The fire at Givray-le-Duc began at the same hour of the same night" (*M*, 310). Although Conchis sees no direct connection, he qualifies himself: "Or rather I am the connection. I am whatever meaning the coincidence has" (*M*, 311). Nicholas concludes that the coincidence is not literally true but believes that through Conchis the two episodes are linked in significance and therefore hold a type of "metaphorical meaning," as the protagonist continues to find "everywhere in the masque, these interrelationships, threads between circumstance" (*M*, 311). Through the sorcery of his narration Conchis thus serves as a didactic demon who connects hell-fire with pillars of fire and continues to both mystify and instruct Nicholas with his interweaving strands of bizarre experience.

Many of Conchis's tales become indirectly didactic in that they expose the various forms of hell created by twentieth-century man. Martin Shuttleworth, for instance, has written about the tableaus that mirror these tales: "each one descend(s) further and further into the under-world of the mind and the century."[25] Like Murdoch and Canetti, Fowles sees links, as Shuttleworth put it, "between the real horrors of our times and the swamps at the bottom of each man's mind."[26] In his story about his younger days as a soldier and his retreat from the Western Front during World War I, Conchis tries to describe the Zeitgeist prior to the war: "So much peace and plenty, for so long a time. In the collective unconscious perhaps everyone wanted a change or purge. A holocaust" (*M*, 117).

This subconscious drift towards disaster leads to the battle of Neuve Chapelle, where the young soldier saw "the bone sticking out of flesh" and recoiled at "the stench of burst intestines" (*M*, 124). Conchis tries to show Nicholas how the world had gone insane:

> The madness of it, Nicholas. Standing in holes in the ground, thou-sands of men, English, Scots, Indians, French, Germans one March morning. . . . Some thirteen thousand killed . . . and all for a few hundred yards of useless mud. . . . If there is a hell, then it is that. Not flames, not pitchforks. But a place without the possibility of reason, like Neuve Chapelle that day. (*M*, 122, 131)

The book descends to even lower depths during Conchis's most sear-ing narration: the account of the German occupation of Phraxos during World War II.[27] Used simply as a lookout, the island is first controlled by Colonel Anton, a civilized and compassionate officer who "shut [his] eyes to countless irregularities" (*M*, 416). But when Greek guerillas shoot four German soldiers who carelessly go swimming, the formerly quiet island turns into a slaughterhouse in hell. In order to "stiffen morale," a certain Colonel Wimmel is dispatched to the island. We are told that Wimmel "had a hand picked company of Teutonic monsters under him, who did the interrogating, torturing, executing, and the rest. They were known, after the badge they wore, as *die Raben*. The Ravens" (*M*, 418). Wimmel's method of dealing with any resistance involves a simple technique: for every German wounded, ten hostages are to be executed; for every German killed, twenty Greeks will be shot. Thus the Greek village owes Wimmel eighty men. Before the executions, however, *die Raben* try to extract information from the five guerillas whom they have captured.

As the town's newly elected mayor, Conchis is led "down the dark stone corridor" to the cellar where *die Raben* are performing their grisly task. Feeling as if he has entered the devil's torture chamber, Conchis says:

> I think any one but a doctor would have fainted. I should have liked to have fainted. The room was bare. In the middle was a table. Roped to the table was a young man [one of the guerillas]. He was naked except for a blood stained singlet, and he had been badly burned about the mouth and eyes. But I could see only one thing. Where his genitals should have been, there was nothing but a black-red hole. They had cut off his penis and scrotal sac. With a pair of wire-cutting shears. . . . There was a disgusting smell of excrement and urine. (*M*, 426)

More shocking scenes follow. As in the earlier war, Conchis concludes, "But there was no reason left in the world. When human beings could do such things to one another" (*M*, 426).

Ironically Wimmel sees his efficient work with *die Raben* as a method of "bringing order into the chaos of Europe" (*M*, 428). Such ideas of order bring to mind some of the more obsessed characters in Murdoch's work. In almost Murdochian imagery, Conchis says of Wimmel: "He was what life could do if it wanted—an extreme possibility made hideously mind and flesh. Perhaps that was why he could impose himself so strongly, like a black divinity. For there was something superhuman in the spell he cast" (*M*, 433).

Largely for propaganda purposes, Wimmel tries to turn Conchis into one of the grim henchmen who creates his mad form of order. He bargains that the eighty Greek hostages will be sent to labor camps rather than be executed if Conchis himself will kill the two guerillas not yet tortured to death by *die Raben*. Feeling he has no choice, Conchis agrees to perform the execution. But when the gun he is handed proves to be empty, he realizes the dimension of Wimmel's insanity: in front of all the villagers Conchis is meant to club the two men to death. In spite of the lives of the eighty hostages, Conchis makes a type of existential choice. He will not join Wimmel and *die Raben* in hell; he chooses for mankind even though eighty men will die. He lays down the gun and stands next to the guerillas who are to be executed.

Although Conchis is hit by the firing squad, his servants later find him still breathing, hide him, and enact a mock funeral. War records subsequently reveal that Wimmel's usual strategy in similar situations involved an apparent last-minute reprieve that was actually followed by only more bloodshed. But this information does not prevent the ghosts of those eighty slain hostages from invading Conchis's nightmares. In spite of his guilt, however, he believes he acted rightly by holding onto the last shred of humanity allowed him.

This ghastly account proves to be the longest and the most riveting of all the tales Conchis narrates. But strangely, one senses that in spite of the depths to which the tale descends, the novel as a whole is elevated to a higher plane. However deceptive his technique, Conchis now appears to be responding to some profoundly moral motivation. Even with his changing masks, he ultimately seems deadly serious, as if he wants all who hear the story to learn its dark lesson to avoid sinking into the miasma the tale explores. One feels that indirectly Conchis is warning Nicholas not to waste life but to attend to the few serious and fundamental concerns of existence.

The protagonist does feel challenged by the somber tale and senses behind it "a moral imperative, an almost Christian concept, certainly not a political or democratic one. I thought back over the last few years of my life, the striving for individuality that had obsessed all my generation after the limiting and conforming years of the war, our retreat from society, nation, into self. I knew I couldn't really answer his charge, the question his story posed; and that I could not get off by claiming that I was a historical victim, powerless to be anything else but selfish" (*M,* 441). Nicholas describes the influence of the hellish narration upon him in terms that seem to echo the theme of demonic didacticism: "It was as if Conchis had planted . . . a succubus on my back: a knowledge I did not want" (*M,* 441).

Even though after the Nazi story the reader senses a decidedly moral purpose behind the masque, Conchis's devious manipulation of Nicholas intensifies. When Nicholas hears that Alison has killed herself, he becomes more dependent upon Julie, who in turn becomes more elusive. Many of the sadistic images from the stories and tableaux coalesce in a scene that combines the various forms of psychological torture inflicted upon Nicholas since his arrival at Bourani. When in desperation Nicholas finally tells members of the masque about Alison's suicide, a special code word is spread among all the players indicating that Conchis's "experiment" is to be stopped immediately. Nicholas is informed that Conchis will be devastated because he is actually a renowned psychiatrist who has been struggling to prevent occurrences such as Alison's death.

Nicholas is finally reunited with Julie, whom Conchis has withheld from him for a painfully long time. Julie admits that she has participated in some of the deceptions but that in one sense she too has been working her way through the labyrinth. Now that the experiment has ended, she acknowledges that she was not always pretending and is indeed strongly attracted to the protagonist. Lightning and a thunderstorm provide an eerie backdrop for the erotic encounter that follows, yet the Circe figure reassures Nicholas that this "is where my witchcraft stops" as she surrenders herself completely to the ardent young man. Nicholas now perceives the previous evasions and tantalizing games as a manifestation of a "paradoxical innocence; Adam and Eve before the Fall" (M, 482). After the two naked lovers have consummated their desire, Nicholas again refers to Paradise as he notices that the thunder has subsided: "All storms were past, and we lay in the silence of Eden regained" (M, 487).

But Nicholas seems to have forgotten that previous moments of heavenly bliss on Bourani were relatively short-lived, and this interlude proves no exception. Almost immediately after making love, "Julie" informs Nicholas that her name isn't Julie, quickly puts on her kimono, hurries to the bedroom door, and lets in a "violent cascade of figures" (M, 488). One critic has called what follows the definitive scene of "Coitus interruptus."[28] Paradise has been lost. When Nicholas sees Conchis and his band of men rush into the bedroom where he lies naked and limp, he thinks: "Flames, devils, hell" (M, 489). Dressed in black, these phantoms of the night apprehend Nicholas, gag him, bind him with ropes, and inject him with drugs.

As the protagonist struggles vainly against these overpowering figures, he identifies with victims in the previous stories and tableaus:

> My mind flashed back to that incident in the war: a room at the end of the corridor, a man lying on his back, castrated. My eyes began to fill with tears of frustrated rage and humiliation. I realized at last what Julie's final look at me had been like. It was that of a surgeon who has just performed a difficult operation successfully; peeling off the rubber gloves, surveying the suture. Trial, flames . . . they were all mad, they must be, and she the most vicious, shameless, degenerate. . . .
> I tried to realize what I had got into: a world of people who knew no laws, no limits.
> A satyr with an arrow in his heart.
> Mirabelle. La Maitress-Machine, a foul engine made fouler flesh.
> (M, 489, 490)

Thus the demonic experiment of Conchis has not ended: once again Paradise has turned into hell; Circe has performed more cruel magic; and in Nicholas's mind Conchis has turned into a Nazi torturer while Julie has evolved into the deadly Mirabelle, who after loving her paramour stabs him in the groin. The cutting imagery associated with the Nazi episode, the references to surgery, Artemis's arrow, and Mirabelle's dagger—all reinforce the idea that the protagonist has undergone an emotional castration. One more time Nicholas is cast into the inferno: "My head began to swim. Faces and objects, the ceiling, receded from present reality; down and down a deep black mine of shock, incomprehension and flailing depths of impossible revenge" (M, 490).

As Nicholas is powerfully subdued by Conchis and his men, he wonders if he is dreaming: "I still couldn't accept the fact that this was not some nightmare, like some freak misbinding in a book, a Lawrence novel become at the turn of a page, one by Kafka" (M, 489). His literary reference becomes even more appropriate when, after being drugged for three days, he finds himself in yet another large underground chamber where he is told there will be a trial. But unlike the inquisition in Kafka's novel, the trial that Conchis arranges is invested with meaning and decidedly moral purpose, which even Nicholas finally starts to realize. Before the didactic intention behind the masque begins to emerge, however, one final scene in the diabolic drama is performed. The setting for the trial suggests esoteric ritual: decorated with burning torches and other cabalistic emblems, the underground room "did not look like a court of justice; but a court of injustice; a Star Chamber" (M, 498). Strapped to a large black chair resembling a throne, Nicholas is soon joined by twelve grotesquely costumed figures out of a nightmare. One by one the grim specters slowly file into a jury box: savage hunters, wolf-men, witches, crocodiles, and a winged vampire with "an eared bat-head in black fur, two long white fangs . . . the clawed wings held rigidly out, bellying a little in the air, uncanny in the torchlight; a great flickering shadow" (M, 499, 500). Other horrors include a pornographic movie laced with sadomasochistic imagery and featuring Julie and a big muscular black man, whom the film labels "Black Bull." Tethered to a wooden frame and forced to watch this obscene film, Nicholas feels "like a voyeur in hell" (M, 529).

Before the trial actually begins, the strangely costumed figures ceremoniously remove their masks. As twenty students with notebooks quietly enter the arena, Nicholas is told that the unmasked players are actually members of a team of international psychologists. Nicholas is then subjected to a cruel public analysis of his psychiatric profile replete with the jargon of modern psychology, such as the observation that the subject suffers from "breast separation traumas" and thus tries to arouse "repressed maternal instincts in his victim which he then proceeds to exploit with semi-incestuous ruthlessness" (*M*, 509). Julie has now become Dr. Vanessa Maxwell, who only briefly glances at Nicholas, as if he were "a diagram on a blackboard" (*M*, 513). Tied and gagged, Nicholas is prevented from releasing the contemptuous scorn he feels for those persecuting him by this embarrassing public evaluation of his psychological history. But he soon learns that he will not be judged by this jury of psychologists—he will instead judge them. And all the wrath he feels will be unleashed upon a scapegoat: Julie's clothes are pulled away from her back; she is tied to a flogging frame; and Nicholas is handed a cat-o'-nine-tails.

Having wanted to spit obscenities during the entire proceedings, now that he is finally ungagged, untied, and given this absolute power, he takes refuge in silence. He slowly begins to realize, as one of Conchis's team later tells him, that Julie was "nothing but a personification of [his] own selfishness" (*M*, 601. He therefore also begins to see that the real demon is lodged not inside a vampire, a witch, or a Nazi torturer, but within his own breast:

> There was a very real devil in me, an evil marquis, that wanted to strike, to see the wet red weals traverse the delicate skin. . . .
> Then suddenly.
> I understood.
> I was not holding a cat in my hand in an underground cistern, I was in a sunlit square ten years before and in my hands I held a German sub-machine gun. And it was not Conchis who was now playing the role of Wimmel. Wimmel was inside me, in my stiffened, back thrown arm, in all my past; above all in what I had done to Alison. (*M*, 517, 518)

Nicholas does not use the cat-o'-nine-tails at his "trial." Although he remains bitter and does not fully understand Conchis and his group's diabolic method of instruction, he senses "a moment of comprehension between all of us, a strange sort of mutual respect . . . a dim conviction of having entered some deeper, wiser esoteric society than I could without danger speak in" (*M*, 519). He, of course, continues to wonder about the real identity of Maurice Conchis and the reasons for such energy and expense in producing the masque. The plot reveals that Conchis is a wealthy man but the source of his income remains unclear. Nicholas once felt that Conchis resembled de Deukans during one period in his life but now has become more socially responsible.[29] The scars on Conchis's body suggest that he too has suffered. And although the earlier narrations could be fabrications, most of the evidence proves that the grisly Nazi episode really did occur. That in itself would qualify as

Conchis's own descent into the underworld. Whatever the specifics of his background, Conchis represents one of the "Few" whom Fowles has written about in *The Aristos*—one of the culturally and morally elite who must assume responsibility for and educate the "Many." He seems to be doing just that, with a method of instruction colored by demonic symbolism and psychology.

The selection of his audience is controlled by chance: whoever gets the job each year as the new English instructor at the Lord Byron School for Boys. The plot uncovers several past instructors, some of them admiring disciples of Conchis, others abject failures and trenchant critics. The fact that Nicholas does not give the game away to the American college student who will be the next English teacher at Phraxos suggests that he ultimately sees the wisdom behind Conchis's hellish system of education.

After being disengaged from the masque, Nicholas plans to leave Greece and return to England. But as a result of his nightmarish journey, the real "place" he will be able to come back to and "know for the first time," as Eliot said, turns out to be Alison—who he learns has not really killed herself. Back in London in the third part of the novel, Nicholas searches desperately to find Alison, but after many futile attempts he simply waits impatiently for her to reappear.

During the book's second section the couple had enjoyed an idyllic interlude on Mount Parnassus. Of course, Nicholas's decision to meet Alison at all was determined by the absence of Conchis and his group from Bourani that weekend. And after the rendezvous on Parnassus, Nicholas could hardly wait to return to the world of the masque. Later when Alison's alleged suicide was reported, he started to cry, "but his tears did not last very long" (*M*, 398). Like Effingham Cooper, he soon began to edge the fact of Alison's suicide "out of the moral world into the aesthetic, where it was easier to live with" (*M*, 401). In what he called a "characteristically twentieth-century retreat from content into form," thoughts of his own disguised self-forgiveness began to coalesce with the idea that Alison's death had in some way ennobled his own life. While contemplating such an idealistic theory, Nicholas also calculated how he would use his grief to evoke Julie's sympathy. Conchis and Julie had been trying all along, of course, to make Nicholas realize the monstrous insensitivity behind such maneuvers.

When Nicholas discovers that Alison did not really die, he concludes that she too has assumed a position on Conchis's expansive stage. Although furious and perplexed, Nicholas desperately wants to see her again. Unsure about whether the masque is still being performed in England, Nicholas walks the tightwire between art and life until the end of the novel. But he has learned to appreciate the reality of Alison's love and believes that she in turn will not be able to hate "someone who's really on his knees. Who'll never be more than half a human being without [her]" (M, 655).

Perhaps Nicholas unconsciously had started to learn the Magus's cruel lesson before he returned to England. Immediately after the brutal Nazi episode, for instance, the protagonist began to think not of Julie but of Alison, whose "death detracted would for ever detract, from my own life. . . . [Since] each death laid a dreadful charge of complicity on the living. . . . I did not pray for her because prayer has no efficacy; I did not cry for her, or for myself because only extroverts cry twice; but I sat in the silence of that night, that infinite hostility to man, to permanence, to love, remembering her, remembering her" (M, 441).

In one sense then Conchis has also yanked Alison down into his underworld. Nicholas comments: "The more I read, the more I began to re-identify the whole situation at Bourani—or at any rate the final situation—with Tartarus. Tartarus was ruled by a king, Hades (or Conchis); a queen, Persephone, bringer of destruction (Lily). . . . And Tartarus was where Eurydice went when Orpheus lost her" (M, 583). The frequent references in the last part of the book to Orpheus and Eurydice suggest that like the unfortunate girl in the myth Alison too is imprisoned in hell and Nicholas must win her back. As he waits in London, he thinks: "Something was expected of me, some Orphean performance that would gain access to the underworld where she was hidden . . . or hiding herself. I was on probation. But no one gave me any real indication of what I was meant to be proving. I had apparently found the entrance to Tartarus. But that brought me no nearer Eurydice" (M, 606). Nicholas's long period of waiting for Alison finally ends when one day he sees her sitting in a tea shop:

> All the time I had expected some spectacular re-entry, some mysterious call, a metaphorical, perhaps even literal descent into a modern Tartarus. And yet, as I stared at her, unable to speak, at her refusal to return my look, I understood that this was the only possible way of return; her rising into the most banal of scenes, this most banal of London, this reality as plain and dull as wheat. Since she was cast as Reality, she had come in her own, yet in some way heightened, stranger, still with the aura of another world; from, but not of, the crowd behind her. (M, 647)

In spite of the wheat imagery, Fowles does not guarantee that the love between Nicholas and Alison will now bloom. Several references to the narrow but deep "abyss" between them hint at a darker alternative. Perhaps the tenuous state of the reunion between Eurydice and Orpheus points to the delicately precise task that will be involved in making the relationship between Alison and Nicholas come to life once again.

Alison's "death" and resurrection after all prove to be more than "tricks" in Conchis's bizarre game: after Nicholas abandoned her, she died emotionally and sank into an underworld of the spirit. Conchis then pulled Nicholas down into hell to make him see that before he assumed the role of Orpheus, his behavior had resembled that of the creature who, according to the myth, had bitten Eurydice and sent her to Hades in the first place: in his cruelty to Alison, Nicholas Urfe had skillfully played the part of the serpent.

The fact that the novel ends on Halloween suggests that the dark spirit of Conchis still looms behind whatever masks Nicholas or Alison may continue to wear. But suddenly the protagonist arrives at the final didactic point behind all the diabolic imagery and possibly speaks for Murdoch and Spark as well as Fowles when he says: "Perhaps it had all been to bring me to this, to give me my last lesson and final ordeal . . . the task . . . of turning lions and unicorns and magi and other mythical monsters into stone statues" (M, 655). The protagonist realizes that the white figures near the park outside the tea shop are simply stone statues, not props in Conchis's theater. Illusion has been replaced by reality; Conchis is no longer watching. Although a final resolution is never reached, Nicholas has learned much from his hellish excursion. He has been taught to see beyond his own solipsistic dramas and can now begin to build a more responsible relationship with Alison in the world outside the masque.

AFTERWORD

Iris Murdoch, Muriel Spark, and John Fowles teach moral lessons in fiction whose symbolic texture is frequently colored by the demonic. Besides appearing in the novels of these three modern British authors, didactic demons have sporadically emerged in other times and places. Christopher Marlowe's Dr. Faustus certainly learns an important lesson from his diabolic visitor. John Milton's Satan teaches profound truths even though he loses Paradise. In their sensational design, the Gothic novels of Ann Radcliffe make strong moral comments by focusing on the plight of the victims enthralled by Satanic villains. In the first half of the twentieth century, pedagogical devils appear in Shaw's *Man and Superman* and C. S. Lewis's *The Screwtape Letters*. Philosophical and playful, these works fail to explore the psychological complexity of demonic obsession rendered so vividly by the three contemporary novelists.

Other recent authors who have combined the demonic with the didactic in isolated works include John Updike in *The Witches of Eastwick*, Anthony Burgess in *The Eve of Saint Venus*, and William Golding in *Lord of the Flies*, whose title provides the meaning of the Hebrew word "Beelzebub."

Contemporary authors often use demonic elements to react to a permissive postwar society. As Anthony Burgess writes, "Nobody sins any more . . . the whole land's . . . a drawing-room in pink cretonne."[1] Many recent writers therefore create hellish imagery to jolt readers into an awareness of real evil—personified in Golding's novel by that ghastly pig's head delivering its diabolic sermon to the mystical Simon. These postwar novels refute the Murdochian character who says: "Modern science has abolished the difference between good and evil."[2]

With the exception of *A Maggot* (depicting both the founder of a religious sect and the Devil), Gothic shadows fall most often throughout the earlier work of John Fowles. His fiction, however, continues to be highly innovative. Although many of Iris Murdoch's ideas remain constant, her style has changed noticeably. Her later works, longer and more leisurely, emulate the expansive nineteenth-century novels that she always considered superior to typically crystalline modern works of fiction.

After comparing her 1986 novel *The Good Apprentice* to several of her earlier books, one must agree with Elizabeth Dipple that in the "protracted subtleties"[3] of her recent technique a new Iris has bloomed. But both Murdoch and Spark have kept close to their original themes late in their careers. In *The Philosopher's Pupil*, Iris Murdoch's 1983 novel, the philosopher maintains, "The holy must try to know the demonic."[4] In Muriel Spark's 1981 novel, *Loitering with Intent,* the heroine confesses, "I was aware of a *daemon* inside me that rejoiced in seeing people as they were."[5] Both works explore mysterious and even supernatural realms of experience.

In certain earlier novels by all three authors strange and charismatic individuals such as Honor Klein *(A Severed Head)*, Douglas Dougal *(The Ballad of Peckham Rye)*, and Maurice Conchis *(The Magus)* are portrayed as diabolic personalities who nevertheless offer moral instruction. These didactic demons are outsiders whose failure to conform to conventional ethics becomes a prerequisite for their attack on the flimsy moral structures society has erected to keep life civilized. Satanic imagery appropriately surrounds these mentors because they force their students to undergo sudden and shocking reevaluations of their lives that plunge the dazed pupils into an underworld of the spirit resembling hell. Martin Lynch-Gibbon, Nicholas Urfe, and the citizens of Peckham Rye must experience a painful journey into their subconscious minds before they can begin to grow into more morally sensitive individuals. All the wine cellars, underground labyrinths, and basement prisons reinforce this idea of a hellish descent into the subconscious regions of the mind.

In a number of works by Murdoch, Spark, and Fowles, moral lessons must be learned without the aid of fictional guides. But in these novels the authors still prove to be didactic as they use demonic imagery to show the obsessive way in which the characters imprison themselves in illusion. In Murdoch's *The Flight from the Enchanter* many of the characters have enslaved themselves to their private fantasies about Mischa Fox so that he becomes a satanic tyrant for those whose submissive personalities bend to his will. In *The Unicorn* characters gaze at Hannah Crean-Smith, but no one really attends to the unique individual locked inside the various myths smothering her within the Gothic milieu of that novel. Spark's *The Public Image* describes an actress caught behind a hideous web of deception that almost strangles her. The servants in *Not to Disturb* no longer recognize the humanity of their masters but think of them only as stepping-stones to new financial security; the cannibalism motif accentuates the way in which human beings prey upon one another in that lurid Swiss chateau. Finally, in John Fowles's first novel the fiendish Clegg looks upon Miranda not as a young woman with changeable moods but only as another specimen in his gruesome collection.

All three authors try to show that the truly "evil eye" is caused by neurotic self-absorption that blurs the vision and prevents the individual from seeing the otherness of people who are not himself. As he fails to recognize their uniqueness, the self-absorbed individual imposes his private fantasies upon other real people. The pervasive mirror and photography imagery frequently symbolizes this deadly solipsistic process. This failure in perception leads to relationships whose obsessive, predatory nature is suggested by metaphors involving prisoners, slaves, and even vampires. Men and women imprison one another in their fantasies; docile servants seek out powerful masters; people suck away energy and vitality in their overwhelming obsessions. Thus whether the character be Nina the dressmaker, Annabel Christopher, Victor Passerat, or Miranda Grey, the victim of this distorted vision often falls into a hellish trap from which there is, as Sartre said, no exit.

NOTES

Overview

1. Sir Charles Snow quoted by Derek Stanford, *Muriel Spark: A Biographical and Critical Study* (Fontwell, Eng,: Centaur Press, 1963), p. 123.
2. Muriel Spark, *The Bachelors* (London: Macmillan, 1961), p. 240.
3. Iris Murdoch in "An Interview with Iris Murdoch," by Michael O. Bellamy, *Contemporary Literature* 18 (1977): 135.
4. Iris Murdoch in "The House of Fiction: Interviews with Seven English Novelists," by Frank Kermode, *Partisan Review* 30 (Spring 1963): 62–65.
5. "Demonology and Dualism: The Supernatural in Isaac Singer and Muriel Spark," in *Critical Views of Isaac Bashevis Singer,* ed. Irvin Malin (New York: New York University Press, 1969), p. 149.
6. "My Conversion," *Twentieth Century* 170 (Autumn 1961): 62.
7. John Fowles, *The Aristos* (Boston: Little, Brown, 1970), p. 21.
8. Ibid., p. 14.
9. Muriel Spark, *The Ballad of Peckham Rye* (Philadelphia: J. B. Lippincott, 1960), p. 115.

Chapter 1. Spellbound

1. Olga M. Meidner, "Reviewer's Bane: A Study of Iris Murdoch's *The Flight from the Enchanter,*" *Essays in Criticism,* 11 (October 1961): 435–47.
2. William Van O'Connor, "Iris Murdoch: The Formal and the Contingent," *Critique* 3 (Winter–Spring 1960): 38.
3. Susan Sontag, "Mind as Passion," *The New York Review of Books* 27, 14, (25 September 1980): p. 47.
4. Elias Canetti, *Crowds and Power* (New York: The Viking Press, 1966), p. 290. (All further references to *Crowds and Power* are to this edition and will be cited within the text as *CP.*)
5. Iris Murdoch, *The Flight from the Enchanter* (New York: The Viking Press, 1956), p. 38. (All further references to *The Flight from the Enchanter* are to this edition and will be cited within the text as *FE.*)
6. Edmund Campion, "A Sort of a Saint," *Quadrant* 22 (July 1978): 58.
7. Sontag, "Mind as Passion," p. 48.
8. Simone Weil, *The Simone Weil Reader,* ed. George A. Panichas (New York: McKay Publishing, 1977), p. 136.
9. Ibid., p. 137.
10. Iris Murdoch, "Against Dryness," *Encounter* 16 (January 1961): 16–20.
11. Frank Baldanza, *Iris Murdoch* (New York: Twayne Publishers, 1974), pp. 52–53.
12. Edith Hamilton, *Mythology* (New York: New American Library, 1969), p. 231.
13. Iris Murdoch, *A Severed Head* (New York: The Viking Press, 1961).

Chapter 2. Phantom Professor

1. Iris Murdoch, *A Severed Head* (New York: The Viking Press, 1961), p. 11. (All further references to *A Severed Head* are to this edition and will be cited within the text as *SH*.)
2. Linda Kuehl, "Iris Murdoch: The Novelist as Magician/The Magician as Artist," *Modern Fiction Studies* 15, 3 (Autumn 1969): 354.
3. A. S. Byatt, *Degrees of Freedom: The Novels of Iris Murdoch* (London: Chatto and Windus, 1965), p. 114.
4. Alan Friedman, *The Turn of the Novel* (New York: Oxford University Press, 1966), pp. 159–78.
5. Jacques Souvage, "The Novels of Iris Murdoch," *Studia Germanica Gardensia* 4 (1962): 247.

Chapter 3. The Evil Eye

1. Leonard Kriegel, "Iris Murdoch: Everybody through the Looking-glass," *Contemporary British Novelists*, ed. Charles Shapiro (Carbondale: Southern Illinois University Press, 1965), p. 75.
2. Iris Murdoch, *The Unicorn* (New York: The Viking Press, 1963), p. 229. (All further references to *The Unicorn* are to this edition and will be cited within the text as *U*.)
3. Rubin Rabinovitz, *Iris Murdoch* (New York: Columbia University Press, 1968), p. 35.
4. W. K. Rose, "An Interview with Iris Murdoch," *Shenandoah* 119 (Winter 1968): 14–15.
5. Ibid., p. 17.
6. Robert Scholes, *The Fabulators* (New York: Oxford University Press, 1967), p. 124.
7. Carl G. Jung, *Psychology and Alchemy*, trans. R. F. C. Hold, in *The Collected Works of C. G. Jung*, 12 (Princeton: Princeton University Press, 1968), p. 436.
8. Ibid., p. 447.
9. Ibid., p. 464.
10. *The Unicorn*, p. 13. Such passages make Frank Baldanza's assessment of Marian as a "common-sense rationalist" (p. 116) seem inaccurate.

Chapter 4. The Intruder

1. Samuel Hynes, "The Prime of Muriel Spark," *Commonweal* 75 (23 February 1962): 563.
2. Carol Murphy, "A Spark of the Supernatural," *Approach* 60 (Summer 1966): 27.
3. Karl Malkoff, *Muriel Spark* (New York: Columbia University Press, 1968), p. 24.
4. Muriel Spark, *The Ballad of Peckham Rye* (Philadelphia: J. B. Lippincott, 1960), pp. 114–15. (All further references to *The Ballad of Peckham Rye* are to this edition and will be cited within the text as *B*.)
5. Malkoff, *Muriel Spark*, p. 23.

Chapter 5. A Visit from the Grave

1. Muriel Spark, *The Bachelors* (London: MacMillan, 1961), p. 117.
2. Ibid., p. 240.

3. Ibid., p. 117.

4. Muriel Spark, *The Public Image* (New York: Alfred A. Knopf, 1968), p. 7. (All further references to *The Public Image* are to this edition and will be cited within the text as *PI*.)

5. Melvin Maddocks, "The Spark Flair for Well-bred Demonology," *Life* (11 October 1968): 10.

6. "*The Public Image* Makes Its Point by Understatement," *National Observer* (9 September 1968); B7.

7. Maddocks, "The Spark Flair," p. 10.

8. "A Novel Snaps the Camera," *Christian Science Monitor* (14 November 1968): 15.

Chapter 6. Hell-House

1. Muriel Spark, *Not to Disturb* (New York: Viking Press, 1972), p. 14. (All further references to *Not to Disturb* are to this edition and will be cited within the text as *ND*.)

2. T. S. Eliot, *The Waste Land* (New York: Harcourt, Brace & World, 1962), p. 34, line 127.

3. "Grub Street Gothic," review of *Not to Disturb*, *Times Literary Supplement* (12 November 1971): 1409.

4. William B. Hill, S. J., review of *Not to Disturb*, *Best Sellers* (15 April 1972): 42–43.

5. Muriel Spark, *The Girls of Slender Means* (New York: Alfred A. Knopf, 1963), p. 174.

6. Patricia Meyer Spacks, review of *Not to Disturb*, *Hudson Review*, 25 (Autumn 1972): 502–3.

7. Ibid., 503.

8. Jonathan Raban, "Vague Scriptures," review of *Not to Disturb*, *New Statesman* (12 November 1971): 657.

9. *Macbeth*, act 2, scene 3.

10. Consider, for instance, "Theology" or "Crow's First Lesson," *The Norton Anthology of Modern Poetry*, ed. Richard Ellmann and Robert O'Clair (New York: W. W. Norton, 1973), pp. 1274, 1977.

11. J. R. Frakes, "Mock-Mod-Gothic," review of *Not to Disturb*, *Washington Post Book World* (16 April 1972): 4.

Chapter 7. A Room without a View

1. Bernard Bergonzi, *The Situation of the Novel* (Pittsburgh, Pa.: University of Pittsburgh Press, 1970), p. 75.

2. "Miranda Removed," review of *The Collector*, *Times Literary Supplement* (17 May 1963): 353.

3. John Ditsky, "The Watch and Chain of Henry James," *University Review* 6, 1 (Fall 1970): 91.

4. *A Severed Head*, p. 12.

5. John Fowles, *The Collector* (Boston: Little, Brown, 1963), p. 3. (All further references to *The Collector* are to this edition and will be cited within the text as *C*).

6. Honor Tracy, "Love under Chloroform," review of *The Collector*, *New Republic* (3 Aug. 1963): 20.

7. Karen Lever, "The Education of John Fowles," *Critique: Studies in Modern Fiction* 21, 2 (1979): 92.

8. John Fowles, "Weeds, Bugs, Americans," *Sports Illustrated* (21 December 1970): 99.

9. William J. Palmer, *The Fiction of John Fowles: Tradition, Art, and the Loneliness of Selfhood* (Columbia: University of Missouri Press, 1974), p. 42.

10. Granville Hicks, "A Caliban with Butterflies," review of *The Collector, Saturday Review* (27 July 1963): 19.

11. Roy Newquist, Interview with John Fowles, *Counterpoint* (New York: Rand McNally, 1964), p. 223.

12. John Mortimer, "Contra Clegg," review of *The Collector* and *The Aristos, New Statesman* (2 July 1965): 16; Paul Pickrel, "Love, Irony, and a Bit of Vitriol," *Harpers Magazine* (August, 1963): 95; Robert Phelps, "The Meek Grub," review of *The Collector, New York Herald Tribune Books* (28 July 1963): 9.

13. Michele Murray, "Twentieth-Century Parable," review of *The Collector, Commonweal* (1 November 1963): 173.

14. John Fowles, *The Aristos* (Boston: Little, Brown, 1970), p. 10.

15. Ibid., pp. 9–11.

16. Tracy, "Love under Chloroform," p. 20.

Chapter 8. Greek Gothic

1. John Fowles, *The Magus: A revised version* (Boston: Little, Brown, 1978), p. 15. (All further references to *The Magus* are to this edition and will be cited within the text as *M*.)
See the following articles for additional commentary on changes in the revised version of *The Magus:* Cory Wade, "'Mystery Enough at Noon': John Fowles's Revision of *The Magus*," *The Southern Review* 15 (1979): 716–23; John Fowles, "*The Magus* Revisited," *London Times* (28 May 1977): 7.

2. Malcolm Bradbury, "The Novelist as Impresario: John Fowles and His Magus," in *Possibilities: Essays on the State of the Novel* (New York: Oxford University Press, 1973), p. 264.

3. Ibid., p. 269.

4. Arthur Edward Waite, *The Pictorial Key to the Tarot* (New York: Causeway Books, 1973), p. 12.

5. P. D. Ouspensky, "The Symbolism of the Tarot" in *A New Model of the Universe* (New York: Alfred A. Knopf, 1967), p. 187.

6. Delma E. Presley, "The Quest of the Bourgeois Hero: An Approach to Fowles' *The Magus*," *Journal of Popular Culture* 6 (Fall 1972): 394–98.

7. Oswald Wirth quoted by Ouspensky, "Symbolism," p. 195.

8. Ouspensky, "Symbolism," p. 195.

9. Ibid., p. 196.

10. Papus, *The Tarot of the Bohemians,* trans. A. P. Morton (London: William Rider & Son, 1919), p. 338.

11. John Fowles, *Islands,* photographs by Fay Godwin (Boston: Little, Brown, 1978), p. 59.

12. *Islands,* p. 56.

13. Ibid. See also: John Fowles, *Shipwreck,* photography by the Gibsons of Scilly (Boston: Little, Brown, 1975); Richard Jeffries, *Bevis: The Story of a Boy* (New York: Everyman's Library, 1966). A secret island plays an important part in this work, which in his foreword to *The Magus* Fowles cites as a significant influence on his novel.

14. *Islands,* p. 74.

15. Ibid., p. 84.

16. Ibid., p. 91.

17. John Fowles, Foreword to *The Magus: A revised version*, p. 9.

18. *Islands*, p. 106.

19. Ibid., p. 95.

20. Ibid., p. 105.

21. Ibid., p. 74.

22. Glendy Culligan, "The Magician and the Bore," review of *The Magus*, *The Reporter* (24 February 1966): 56.

23. James R. Lindroth, review of *The Magus*, *America* (12 February 1966): 234.

24. John Fowles, "The Trouble with Starlets," *Holiday* 39 (June 1966): 18.

25. Martin Shuttleworth, review of *The Magus*, *Punch* (4 May 1966): 668.

26. Ibid.

27. A biographical approach to Fowles can be revealing. One might consider the Nazi episode that follows in light of the author's comment about his job as a headboy at Bedford, an elite English prep school: "It was one of those schools where a clique of senior boys are given complete license to discipline (i.e., tyrannize) the rest. I was chief of a Gestapo-like network of prefects (student monitors), and each day I was both judge and executioner of a long queue of criminals. Even then only half of me believed in this beastly system; but it was a fortunate experience. By the age of eighteen I had dominion over six hundred boys, and learnt all about power, hierarchy, and the manipulation of law. Ever since I have had a violent hatred of leaders, organizers, bosses: of anyone who thinks it good to get or have arbitrary power over other people." John Fowles quoted in *Current Biography* 38 (March 1977): 160.

28. Thomas Churchill, "Waterhouse, Storey, and Fowles: Which Way Out of the Room?" *Critique: Studies in Modern Fiction*, 10, 3 (1968): 87.

29. Several critics have recognized the mirror images in Conchis's tales. When he met de Deukans, Conchis was twenty-five, Urfe's age when he arrived at Bourani. Both older men then take the younger men on a tour of their respective chateaus. As Peter Wolfe comments, "These echoes or hauntings emphasize the moral lessons embedded in Conchis's narratives." For an extension of this argument see: Peter Wolfe, *John Fowles, Magus and Moralist* (Lewisburg, Pa.: Bucknell University Press, 1976), pp. 109–11.

Afterword

1. Anthony Burgess, *The Eve of Saint Venus* (New York: W. W. Norton, 1970), pp. 48, 98.

2. Iris Murdoch, *The Good Apprentice* (New York: The Viking Press, 1986), p. 29.

3. Elizabeth Dipple, *Iris Murdoch: Work for the Spirit* (Chicago: University of Chicago Press, 1982), pp. 306–48. Published before *The Good Apprentice* was written, Dipple's comprehensive yet penetrating study nevertheless focuses in its last chapter on the "languorous extensions" of other later works such as *The Sea, The Sea* and *Nuns and Soldiers*.

4. Iris Murdoch, *The Philosopher's Pupil* (New York: The Viking Press, 1983), p. 196.

5. Muriel Spark, *Loitering with Intent* (New York: Coward, McCann, & Geoghegan, 1981), p. 10.

BIBLIOGRAPHY

John Fowles

A. WORKS BY FOWLES

Fiction

The Collector, Boston: Little, Brown, 1963.
The Magus. Boston: Little, Brown, 1966.
The French Lieutenant's Woman. Boston: Little, Brown, 1969.
The Ebony Tower. Boston: Little, Brown, 1974.
Daniel Martin. Boston: Little, Brown, 1977.
The Magus: a revised version. Boston: Little, Brown, 1978.
Mantissa. Boston: Little, Brown, 1982.
A Maggot. Boston: Little, Brown, 1985.

Essays and Articles

"I Write, Therefore I Am." *Evergreen Review,* 33 (August–September 1964): 16–17, 89–91.
"The Trouble with Starlets." *Holiday* 39 (June 1966): 12–20.
"Notes on Writing." *Harpers* 237 (July 1968): 88–90.
The Aristos. Boston: Little, Brown, 1970.
"My Recollections of Kafka." *Mosaic* 4 (Summer 1970): 31–41.
"Weeds, Bugs, Americans." *Sports Illustrated* (December 1970): pp. 84–102.
Shipwreck, Photography by the Gibsons of Scilly. Boston: Little, Brown, 1975.
"The Magus Revisited." *London Times* (28 May 1977): 7.
Islands. Photography by Fay Godwin. Boston: Little, Brown, 1978.

B. CRITICISM AND RELATED GENERAL SOURCES

Austen, Jane. *Emma.* New York: Dodd Mead, 1961.
Bergonzi, Bernard. *The Situation of the Novel.* Pittsburgh, Pa.: University of Pittsburgh Press, 1970.
Bradbury, Malcolm. *Possibilities: Essays on the State of the Novel.* New York: Oxford University Press, 1973.
Campbell, James. "An Interview with John Fowles." *Contemporary Literature,* 18 (Autumn 1976): 455–69.

Churchill, Thomas. "Waterhouse, Storey, and Fowles: Which Way Out of the Room?" *Critique: Studies in Modern Fiction,* 10, 3 (1968): 72–87.

Culligan, Glendy. "The Magician and the Bore." Review of *The Magus. The Reporter* (24 February 1966): 56, 58.

Ditsky, John. "The Watch and Chain of Henry James." *University Review,* 6, 1 (Fall 1970): 91–101.

Gardner, John. *On Moral Fiction.* New York: Basic Books, 1978.

Halpern, Daniel. "A Sort of Exile in Lyme Regis." Interview with John Fowles. *London Magazine* (March 1971): 34–46.

Hicks, Granville. "A Caliban with Butterflies." Review of *The Collector. Saturday Review* (27 July 1963): 19.

Jeffries, Richard. *Bevis: The Story of A Boy.* New York: Everyman's Library, 1966.

"John Fowles." *Current Biography Yearbook,* 1977. Edited by Charles Moritz. New York: H. W. Wilson Company, 1977, pp. 159–63.

Lattimore, Richard, trans. *The Odyssey of Homer.* New York: Harper & Row, 1967.

Lever, Karen. "The Education of John Fowles." *Critique: Studies in Modern Fiction,* 21, 2 (1979): 85–99.

Lindroth, James R. Review of *The Magus. America* (12 February 1966): 234.

"Miranda Removed." Review of *The Collector. Times Literary Supplement* (17 May 1963): 353.

Mortimer, John. "Contra Clegg." Review of *The Collector* and *The Aristos. New Statesman* (2 July 1965): 16.

Murray, Michele. "Twentieth-Century Parable." Review of *The Collector. Commonweal* (1 November 1963): 172–73.

Newquist, Roy. Interview with John Fowles. In his *Counterpoint.* New York: Rand McNally, 1964, pp. 218–25.

Ouspensky, P. D. "The Symbolism of the Tarot." In his *A New Model of the Universe.* New York: Alfred A. Knopf, 1967, pp. 186–215.

Palmer, William J. *The Fiction of John Fowles: Traditon, Art, and the Loneliness of Selfhood.* Columbia: University of Missouri Press, 1974.

Papus. *The Tarot of the Bohemians.* Translated by A. P. Morton. London: William Rider & Son, 1919.

Phelps, Robert. "The Meek Grub." Review of *The Collector. New York Herald Tribune Books* (28 July 1963): 9.

Pickrel, Paul. "Love, Irony, and a Bit of Vitriol." Review of *The Collector. Harpers Magazine* 227 (August 1963): 95–96.

Presley, Delma E. "The Quest of the Bourgeois Hero: An Approach to Fowles' *The Magus." Journal of Popular Culture,* 6 (Fall 1972): 394–98.

Shuttleworth, Martin. Review of *The Magus. Punch* (4 May 1966): 668.

Tracy, Honor. "Love under Chloroform." Review of *The Collector. New Republic* (3 August 1963): 20–21.

Wade, Cory. " 'Mystery Enough at Noon': John Fowles's Revision of *The Magus." The Southern Review* 15 (1979): 716–23.

Waite, Arthur Edward. *The Pictorial Key to the Tarot.* New York: Causeway Books, 1973.

Wolfe, Peter. *John Fowles, Magus and Moralist.* Lewisburg, Pa.: Bucknell Unversity Press, 1976.

Iris Murdoch

A. WORKS BY MURDOCH

Fiction

Under the Net. New York: Viking Press, 1954.
The Flight from the Enchanter. New York: Viking Press, 1956.
The Sandcastle. New York: Viking Press, 1957.
The Bell. New York: Viking Press, 1958.
A Severed Head. New York: Viking Press, 1961.
An Unofficial Rose. New York: Viking Press, 1962.
The Unicorn. New York: Viking Press, 1963.
The Italian Girl. New York: Viking Press, 1964.
The Red and the Green. New York: Viking Press, 1965.
The Time of the Angels. New York: Viking Press, 1966.
The Nice and the Good. New York: Viking Press, 1968.
Bruno's Dream. New York: Viking Press, 1969.
A Fairly Honourable Defeat. New York: Viking Press, 1970.
An Accidental Man. New York: Viking Press, 1972.
The Black Prince. New York: Viking Press, 1973.
The Sacred and Profane Love Machine. New York: Viking Press, 1974.
A Word Child. New York: Viking Press, 1975.
Henry and Cato. New York: Viking Press, 1977.
The Sea, the Sea. New York: Viking Press, 1978.
Nuns and Soldiers. New York: Viking Press, 1981.
The Philosopher's Pupil. New York: Viking Press, 1983.
The Good Apprentice. New York: Viking Press, 1986.

Essays

"The Novelist as Metaphysician." *The Listener,* 43 (16 March 1950); 473–76.
"The Existential Hero." *The Listener,* 43 (23 March 1950): 523–24.
"Metaphysics and Ethics," *The Nature of Metaphysics.* Edited by D. F. Pears. London: Macmillan, 1957.
"A House of Theory." *Partisan Review,* 26 (1959): 17–31.
"The Sublime and the Good." *Chicago Review* 13 (Autumn 1959): 42–55.
"The Sublime and the Beautiful Revisited." *Yale Review* 49 (1959): 42–55.
"Against Dryness: A Polemical Sketch." *Encounter,* 16 (January 1961): 16–20.
"The Darkness of Practical Reason." *Encounter,* 27 (July 1966): 46–50.
"Existentialists and Mystics," *Essays and Poems Presented to Lord David Cecil.* Ed. W. Robson. London: Constable, 1970.

Books of Philosophy

Sartre: Romantic Rationalist. New Haven, Conn.: Yale University Press, 1953.
The Sovereignty of Good. London: Routledge and Kegan Paul, 1970.

The Fire and the Sun: Why Plato Banished the Artists. Oxford: Oxford University Press, 1977.

Acastos: Two Platonic Dialogues. New York: Viking Press, 1987.

B. CRITICISM AND RELATED GENERAL SOURCES

Baldanza, Frank. *Iris Murdoch.* New York: Twayne Publishers, 1974.

Bellamy, Michael O. "An Interview with Iris Murdoch." *Contemporary Literature* 18 (1977): 129–40.

Byatt, A. S. *Degrees of Freedom: The Novels of Iris Murdoch.* London: Chatto and Windus, 1965.

Campion, Edmund. "A Sort of a Saint." *Quadrant* 22 (July 1978): 58–60.

Canetti, Elias. *Crowds and Power.* New York: Viking Press, 1963.

Conradi, Peter J. *Iris Murdoch: The Saint and the Artist.* New York: St. Martin's Press, 1986.

Dipple, Elizabeth. *Iris Murdoch: Work for the Spirit.* Chicago: University of Chicago Press, 1982.

Friedman, Alan. *The Turn of the Novel.* New York: Oxford University Press, 1966.

Hague, Angela. *Iris Murdoch's Comic Vision.* Selinsgrove, Pa.: Susquehanna University Press, 1983.

Hamilton, Edith, *Mythology.* New York: New American Library, 1969.

Jung, Carl G. *Psychology and Alchemy,* Translated by R. F. C. Hold. In *The Collected Works of C. G. Jung,* vol. 12. Princeton University Press, 1968.

Kermode, Frank. "The House of Fiction: Interviews with Seven English Novelists." *Partisan Review* 30 (Spring 1963): 62–65.

Kriegal, Leonard. "Iris Murdoch: Everybody through the Looking-glass." In *Contemporary British Novelists,* edited by Charles Shapiro, pp. 62–80. Carbondale: Southern Illinois University Press, 1965.

Kuehl, Linda. "Iris Murdoch: The Novelist as Magician/The Magician as Artist." *Modern Fiction Studies* 15, 3 (Autumn 1969): 347–60.

Meidner, Olga M. "Reviewer's Bane: A Study of Iris Murdoch's *The Flight from the Enchanter.*" *Essays in Criticism* 11 (October 1961): 435–47.

O'Connor, William Van. "Iris Murdoch: The Formal and the Contingent." *Critique* 3 (Winter–spring 1960): 30–36.

Rabinovitz, Rubin. *Iris Murdoch.* New York: Columbia University Press, 1968.

Rose, W. K. "An Interview with Iris Murdoch." *Shenandoah* 19 (Winter 1968): 3–22.

Scholes, Robert. "Iris Murdoch's *Unicorn.*" In his *The Fabulators,* pp. 106–32. New York: Oxford University Press, 1967.

Sontag, Susan. "Mind as Passion." *The New York Review of Books* 27, 14 (25 September 1980): 47–52.

Souvage, Jacques. "The Novels of Iris Murdoch." *Studia Germanica Gardensia* 4 (1962): 225–52.

Sullivan, Zohreh T. "The Contracting Universe of Iris Murdoch's Gothic Novels." *Modern Fiction Studies* 23 (1977–78): 557–69.

Weil, Simone. *The Simone Weil Reader.* Edited by George A. Panichas. New York: McKay Publishing, 1977.

Wolfe, Peter. *The Disciplined Heart: Iris Murdoch and Her Novels.* Columbia: University of Missouri Press, 1966.

Muriel Spark

A. WORKS BY SPARK

Fiction

The Comforters. Philadelphia: J. B. Lippincott, 1957.
Memento Mori. Philadelphia: J. B. Lippincott, 1959.
Robinson. Philadelphia: J. B. Lippincott, 1958.
The Ballad of Peckham Rye. Philadelphia: J. B. Lippincott, 1960.
The Bachelors. London: Macmillan, 1961.
The Prime of Miss Jean Brodie. Philadelphia: J. B. Lippincott, 1962.
The Girls of Slender Means. New York: Alfred A. Knopf, 1963.
The Mandelbaum Gate. New York: Alfred A. Knopf, 1965.
The Public Image. New York: Alfred A. Knopf, 1968.
The Driver's Seat. New York: Alfred A. Knopf, 1970.
Not to Disturb. New York: Alfred A. Knopf, 1972.
The Hothouse by the East River. New York: Viking Press, 1973.
The Abbess of Crewe: A Modern Morality Tale. New York: Viking Press, 1974.
The Takeover. New York: Viking Press, 1976.
Territorial Rights. London: Macmillan, 1979.
Loitering with Intent. New York: Coward, McCann, & Geoghegan, 1981.
The Only Problem. New York: Coward, McCann, & Geoghegan, 1984.

Articles

"My Conversion." *Twentieth Century* 170 (Autumn 1961): 58–63.
"How I Became a Novelist." *Books and Bookmen* 7 (November 1961): 9.
"My Rome." *The New York Times Magazine,* Part 2 (13 March 1983): 36, 39, 70, 72.

Biography

Mary Shelley: A Biography. New York: E. P. Dutton, 1987.

B. CRITICISM AND RELATED GENERAL SOURCES

Berthoff, Warner. "Fortunes of the Novel: Muriel Spark and Iris Murdoch." *Massachusetts Review* 8 (Spring 1967): 301–32.
Burgess, Anthony. *The Eve of Saint Venus.* New York: W. W. Norton, 1979.
Eliot, T. S. *The Waste Land.* New York: Harcourt, Brace & World, 1962.
Ellmann, Richard, and Robert O'Clair, eds. *The Norton Anthology of Modern Poetry.* New York: W. W. Norton, 1973.
Frakes, J. R. "Mock-Mod-Gothic." Review of *Not to Disturb. Washington Post Book World* (16 April 1972): 4.
Frankel, Hashel. "Grub Street Gothic." Review of *Not to Disturb. Times Literary Supplement* (12 November 1971): 1409.
Hill, William B. Review of *Not to Disturb. Best Sellers* (15 April 1972): 42–43.

Hynes, Samuel. "The Prime of Muriel Spark." *Commonweal* 75 (23 February 1962): 562–63, 567–68.

Karl, Frederick R. *A Reader's Guide to the Contemporary English Novel,* Rev. ed. Toronto: Doubleday, Canada 1972.

Kiely, Robert. "A Novel Snaps the Camera." Review of *The Public Image. Christian Science Monitor* (14 November 1968): 15.

Maddocks, Melvin. "The Spark Flair for Well-bred Demonology." *Life* (11 October 1968): 10.

Malkoff, Karl. *Muriel Spark.* New York: Columbia University Press, 1968.

———. "Demonology and Dualism: The Supernatural in Isaac Singer and Muriel Spark." In *Critical Views of Isaac Bashevis Singer,* edited by Irvin Malin, pp. 149–68. New York: New York University Press, 1969.

Murphy, Carol. "A Spark of the Supernatural." *Approach* 60 (Summer 1966): 26–30.

Ostermann, Robert. "*The Public Image* Makes Its Point by Understatement." Review of *The Public Image. National Observer* (9 September 1968): B7.

Phelps, Robert. "With a Happy Touch of the Brimstone." Review of *The Ballad of Peckham Rye. New York Herald Tribune Book Review* 7 (August 1960): 3.

Raban, Jonathan. "Vague Scriptures." Review of *Not to Disturb. New Statesman* 82 (12 November 1971): 657–58.

Spacks, Patricia Meyer. Review of *Not to Disturb. Hudson Review* 25 (Autumn 1972): 502–3.

Shakespeare, William. *Macbeth.* In *Shakespeare: The Complete Works,* edited by G. B. Harrison. New York: Harcourt, Brace & World, 1952.

Stanford, Derek. *Muriel Spark: A Biographical and Critical Study.* Fontwell, Eng.: Centaur Press, 1963.

Tominaga, Thomas T., and Wilma Schneidermeyer. *Iris Murdoch and Muriel Spark: A Bibliography.* Metuchen, N.J.: The Scarecrow Press, 1976.

INDEX